LIVING

"Does life control us or do we control life? This book will help us regain positive control of our lives. I recommend it."
Laurence Singlehurst, Director, YWAM England

"A practical and biblical guide to finding God's mission statement for your life and aligning yourself to God's purpose. This is essential reading for all believers who truly want to put first things first."
Rev. Dr Mark Stibbe, author, and Vicar of St Andrew's, Chorleywood

"The rarest and most sought-after commodity in the world today is neither gold nor platinum: it is purpose. Without a sense of purpose, all the wealth in the world won't satisfy. With a sense of purpose, the worst of deprivations can be endured. Tom and Christine Sine have done our culture a great service by reminding us of this and by offering us sensitive and creative ways to get off the treadmill of meaningless acquisition and into a purposeful life. Their style, as ever, is fast-moving, readable and entertaining, and their own sense of purpose – to help Christians worldwide towards a God-centred, shalom-filled celebratory life – breaks through on every page.

"Building a lifestyle you can't enjoy is like buying a coat that is fashionable: expensive and head-turning, but too stiff and heavy to wear. And yet Christians all over the West are doing just that: breaking their necks for a lifestyle that, in the end, leaves them empty. Tom and Christine go back to an ancient story to find the antidote to this fever, and to connect us once more with the purposes of God. They are relentless in their pursuit of this one goal: to help us to understand that the life God calls us to is a life of celebratory self-giving. Offering radical therapy for victims of the affluenza epidemic that has swept through the church, this book will help many ordinary Christians to make a dynamic connection with the purposes of God for their lives."
Gerard Kelly, author of
Get a Grip on the Future without Losing Your Hold on the Past

"This book arrived just on time for me! This week I've been reviewing my schedule, and trying to escape from the 'hurry sickness' which is tying my system in knots! This book is a must for busy Christians who are trying to discover what it means to live lives that are fruitful, not tarnished with stress, exhaustion and over-scheduling!"

The Rev. Dr Rob Frost, author, evangelist and broadcaster

Dr Tom Sine is a futurologist, who specialises in assisting Christian churches and organisations to face coming challenges and opportunities. He is the author of a number of successful books, most recently *Mustard Seed Versus McWorld*.

Dr Christine Sine is a medical doctor who set up the medical work aboard the YWAM mercy ship *Anastasis*. She is author of *Confessions of a Seasick Doctor*. The Sines live in Seattle, Washington, and are frequent visitors to the UK.

Living on Purpose

Finding God's Best for Your Life

TOM AND CHRISTINE SINE

**MONARCH
BOOKS**
Mill Hill, London

Copyright © Tom and Christine Sine 2002.
The right of Tom and Christine Sine to be identified
as authors of this work has been asserted by them
in accordance with the Copyright, Designs
and Patents Act 1988.

First published in 2002 by Monarch Books,
Concorde House, Grenville Place, Mill Hill,
London, NW7 3SA, UK.

ISBN 1 85424 520 1

Unless otherwise stated, Scripture quotations are
taken from *The New International Version*, copyright © 1973, 1978,
1984 by the International Bible Society.

British Library Cataloguing Data
A catalogue record for this book is available
from the British Library.

Book design and production for the publishers by
Bookprint Creative Services
P.O. Box 827, BN21 3YJ, England.
Printed in Great Britain.

Contents

Acknowledgments

Living on Purpose: Finding God's Best was really a group effort. Since the book was written to provide a practical step by step approach to helping Christians put first things first we asked a lot of our friends and associates to read along and help us stay on target. We want to thank Tom Balke, Richard Kew, Ed Smith, Steve Hoke, Dick Towner, John Frank, Paula Harris, Mike Morris, Michael Reeves, Bryan Burton, Mark Mayhle, Rob Shuler, Bruce Bishop, Edgar Stoesz, James B. Notkin, Andy and Helen Harrington, Mat Sciba, Tom Patterson, Gary Heard and Mark Pierson for their helpful input.

Christine and I are particularly indebted to our small group: Stan Thornburg, Coe and Janet Hutchison, and Don and Patty Doty for their support during these days of drafting and re-writing. And we are grateful for the prayers and encouragement of our friends at Saint Albans Episcopal Church and our pastor and his wife Dorsey and Betsy McConnell. Frankly, we couldn't have completed the project without the constant help and support of our administrative assistants at Mustard Seed Associates: Mary Pan, Valerie Norwood and Aimee Buchholz.

This is the first time Christine and I have written a book together and I want to express deep appreciation not only for her creativity and long hours of investment but her remarkable patience with her troublesome husband. In retrospect we feel this challenging project has actually brought us closer together and reinforced our desire to seek first something of God's new order in our own lives, marriage and ministry together through MSA.

Living on Purpose is dedicated to all those friends of Jesus, in many different countries, who are taking the risk of doing what he did and committing their lives to seeking first the purposes of God and discovering life with a difference.

Introduction

The high costs of high-speed living

Recently we were driving along the motorway back to Seattle when it began to rain – not an unusual occurrence in our part of the world! But suddenly the rain came down in torrents, which is unusual. It was a downpour that would have impressed Noah. We slowed to 25 miles an hour in the almost zero visibility, watching with amazement as other drivers zoomed past at 65 to 80 miles an hour. Suddenly we slammed on the brakes and skidded to a halt. We narrowly missed colliding with the car ahead.

Some of those drivers who had sped by weren't as fortunate. Over the next hour we slowly threaded our way through the 45-car pile up of those who had been in a hurry. Glass and broken metal littered the highway and occupants huddled in stunned groups beside what was left of their cars. At the front of the pile up the emergency crew huddled around an overturned car. Beside it lay a body on a stretcher cloaked in a white sheet.

All of us know that speed kills. However we have become obsessed with high-speed living and the desire to save time. When the unexpected hits we end up in the middle of a disaster over which we have no control at all . . . and we become victims of our own hurried and harried lives.

Where does our drivenness come from?

Many of us dash along the motorways of our lives at a mad pace too. "Hurry" for too many of us is becoming the defining

7

characteristic of our lives. We dash frantically from job, to home to church. Even Christians aren't immune. A recent bumper sticker we read said: *Jesus is Coming Back . . . Look Busy!* And most of us not only look busy, we are drowning in busyness. In the back of our minds a small nagging voice keeps asking "Is this what life is really meant to be about?" "Is this the best that life has to offer?" "Why have so many of our lives become so driven?"

A friend of ours in the Dominican Republic was watching the monumental film *The Titanic* recently with Spanish subtitles and a very energetic audience. As the Titanic began to sink the young heroine, Kate Winslet, and hero, Leonardo Di Caprio, were hanging over the side literally by their fingernails. Huge waves reached up to consume them. As Rose turned to Jack in evident desperation the by-line flashed up on the screen, "Que paso Jack?" The audience roared. Something obviously got lost in the translation. But seriously, do you ever find yourself hanging by your fingernails wondering what's happening and how you got into this fix?

Why are many of us in such a hurry? We believe one of the major reasons is that we have unwittingly allowed others to define what is best for our lives. A number of men and increasingly women too allow their work to define their sense of purpose. Take Ed for example. He works for a corporation and spends half his life travelling. At home Ed is constantly on his cell phone and rarely takes a day off. His wife feels he is more familiar with the inside of a plane than with their own home. Ed's drivenness comes from his unquestioning acceptance that the overarching purpose of life is about getting ahead in his career. Family, friends and church share the bare leftovers of Ed's driven life. Perhaps you know someone in your church like Ed.

For others the pressures of family life and the expectations of the suburbs define the direction of their lives. Lois is totally invested in her kids and enabling them to be high achievers in their upscale suburban neighbourhood. As a consequence she has signed her two girls up for a range of activities from music lessons to modelling classes. Lois has never noticed that she has allowed her neighbourhood's expectations about what constitutes "high achievement" and the good life to define not only the direction of her family's life but to chart her daughters' futures too. Nor has she realized that, though she and her family are active in the church, their faith has almost nothing to do with the direction of their lives . . . but it does add to their busyness.

In quest of the best

Many of us can relate to the line in one of Bruce Cockburn's songs, "He tried to build the New Jerusalem and ended up with New York!" We started our lives with a lot of idealism headed towards God's New Jerusalem and then woke up one morning finding ourselves caught up in a very frenetic New York City kind of lifestyle and we are exhausted.

The premise of *Living on Purpose . . . Finding God's Best for Your Life* is that we are convinced you want to find a less stressed more satisfying way of life . . . a way of life that counts for something. We believe you want the best God has for you and your loved ones. The tragedy is that too many of us settle for less, much less, and we miss God's best. We miss God's best because we have little sense of how to find a direction and a rhythm for our lives that flows directly out of our faith. Failing to find a compelling sense of direction from our faith, like Ed and Lois, too often we unwittingly allow others to define both the purpose and the pace of our lives. Many of us wind up exhausted and unfulfilled. The question we fail to ask is "Why does our faith seem to have so little influence in defining both the direction and tempo of our lives?"

We are convinced that our faith has so little influence on the direction and tempo of our lives primarily because of a serious and largely undiscussed disconnect between our daily life and our Sunday faith. We often tell pastors "People in your churches have absolutely no idea how to connect whatever is preached on Sunday morning to how they spend their time and resources Monday through Saturday."

Making the connect between God's purposes and our lives

In this book we not only want to help you find a connect between Sunday faith and daily life, we also want you to find the enormous satisfaction of *living on purpose*. We dare not underestimate the power of purpose to shape our lives for better or worse. Richard Leider, writing for corporate leaders, states, "Purpose is that deepest dimension within us – our central core or essence – where we have a profound sense of who we are, where we came from, and where we are going."[1]

As people committed to an ancient faith we will never be satisfied if we allow the driven purposes of modern culture to define our direction or set our tempo. We will only find the best that God has for us by rediscovering in the Great Story a profound sense of who we are, where we came from, and where we are going. It is only as we merge our story with God's story that we can find the purpose for life we seek and a rhythm of life that is renewing instead of exhausting.

Syd Hielema, a professor of theology at Dordt College, Iowa, points out that we all have the opportunity to become a part of The Story that begins in the Garden and will be consummated in the New Creation. He writes invitingly "We are all like actors in a play . . . and we are told, 'here is your script. You know the character and the plotline . . . Improvise your parts in the drama so that what you do is consistent with everything I have revealed to you about this drama'."[2] In other words not only does the Author invite us to be a part of this drama but we are also invited to improvise how we blend our story with God's story. If we accept this invitation we will find direction for our lives that comes directly from God's story instead of the driven aspirations of modern culture.

Jesus was born into a world that, like ours, had two dominating stories. One was a story of self-interest and commerce in an oppressive Roman world. The other was a story of an ancient Jewish faith that began with Abraham and Sarah and which scripture teaches is destined to transform the world. As he grew into adulthood Jesus lived in both stories and both worlds. But he made a very conscious choice not only to embrace the second story as "The Story" but to make God's purposes his purposes. The mission statement he chose for his life came from Isaiah 61: "The Spirit of the Lord is on me because he has anointed me to preach good news to the poor. He has sent me to proclaim freedom for the prisoners and recovery of sight for the blind, to release the oppressed, to proclaim the year of the Lord's favor" (Luke 4:18–19).

Many of those first disciples and millions of others over the centuries have chosen, like Jesus, to commit their lives not only to God but also to the purposes of God. They found God's best by turning their backs on the purposes of the dominant culture and giving their lives to the purposes of God's kingdom. Over and over again we read that those who found God's best for their lives, from Francis of Assisi to John Wesley, were used by God to make an extraordinary difference in their world, just like the One they followed. God is still inviting disciples to discover the difference their lives can make if they, like Jesus, make God's purposes their purposes.

Finding the focus

The intention of this book is to enable you to find God's best for your life . . . *living on purpose*. We want to help you find a strong connect between your Sunday faith and your life seven days a week. We want to enable you to find a way of life with a difference that begins with the story of God . . . a way of life that is more satisfying and less exhausting than anything the stress-race can offer. We will show how you begin *living on purpose* by doing what Jesus did . . . using scripture to discover a mission statement for your life. Once you have drafted a mission statement we will show you how to use that statement to create a more celebrative way of life that makes a difference in the world in ways you never imagined.

Remembering the possibilities of the mustard seed

Jesus let us in on an astonishing secret. God has chosen to change the world through the lowly, the unassuming, and the imperceptible.[3] Jesus said, "What shall we say the kingdom of God is like, or what parable shall we use to describe it? It is like a mustard seed, which is the smallest seed you plant in the ground. Yet when planted, it grows and becomes the largest of garden plants, with such big branches that the birds of the air can perch in its shade" (Mark 4:30–32). God is still using the foolish things of the earth to confound the mighty – which should give us all hope. The Bible teaches that God is still working through ordinary people to make a kingdom difference in our world.

Checking out the road map

This book is intended to provide a practical creative way to enable *you* to journey with us to find God's best and to make God's purposes your purposes. It is designed to be used by individuals or couples but probably has greatest value if it is used by small groups or Sunday school classes as an eight-week curriculum. It is also designed to be used as a college or Bible school textbook in courses on applied faith. We include two "off ramps" in every chapter where you have the opportunity to pull off to the side and actually apply these principles to your life. During these exercises we will enable you not only to draft a biblical mission statement but also to put wheels under it and create the more satisfying way of life you are seeking.

The whole idea of life as a journey is basic to Christianity. In the Middle Ages pilgrimage became a popular expression of a

Christian's whole faith experience and a way to enter more fully into God's story. Devout and humble believers often spent months trekking to some holy shrine as a symbol of their journey toward the City of God and away from the appetites and addictions of the world. In the first two chapters we contrast two very different stories about our world with two very different visions for what constitutes the good life and the better future. One story is about Boom City, the other the City of Shalom. In Chapter Three we will discover how to use a biblical sense of God's purposes to draft a personal mission statement to begin re-focusing our lives.

In succeeding chapters we will outline imaginative ways you can use your mission statements to reinvent your lifestyles and timestyles to reflect more authentically the purposes and rhythms of God's Shalom kingdom. In this journey together we hope to help you discover a more festive, less stressed way of life in which you see how God can use you to make a difference in your world.

Why another book on mission statements?

Let's be clear. There is no shortage of books on mission statements. But we have found virtually no books on the topic that use scripture seriously to enable believers to find purpose for their lives. Most of the books we have reviewed tend to start with what turns us on instead of asking what God's purposes are and how we can incorporate those purposes in our lives.

Stephen Covey's bestseller *The 7 Habits of Highly Effective Families* is a very useful book on mission statements that starts by asking "What kind of family do we really want to be?"[4] For a secular audience this is a great question to begin with, but those of us who are Christians must start with a prior question: "What kind of people does God want us to be and how does God want us to be involved both as individuals and families in the work of God's kingdom?"

In Laurie Beth Jones' helpful book *The Path* she stresses the importance of developing mission statements to enable us to clarify our purpose and reconsider our life priorities. But she also begins with "me": what I want, what makes me unique and what stirs my passions . . . instead of beginning with what God wants and how my uniqueness and my passions can become a part of God's agenda.[5]

We are convinced that God cares for us very deeply. God has purposes for all of us that are far more satisfying and rewarding than the drivenness and exhaustion which characterize too many of our lives. And in the life God maps out, we will discover, there is time for God, for family and friends, for celebration and recreation as well as for caring for others. There is even time to just sit and soak in the beauty of God's wonderful creation. You will join Christians all over the world who are a part of God's story that is quietly changing our world. We will particularly share what God is doing through a new generation of Christians. So buckle up your seat belts and let's begin our journey. Let us know on www.msainfo.org how the journey toward *living on purpose* goes for you.

Notes

1. Richard D. Leider, *The Power of Purpose: Creating Meaning in Your Life and Work*, San Francisco: Berrett-Koehler, 1997, p. 1.
2. Syd Hielema, *Improvising Inside the Whole Story*, pp. 1–6, presented at B. J. Haan Educators' Conference, Dordt College, March 2000.
3. Tom Sine, *The Mustard Seed Conspiracy*, Waco: Word Books, 1981, p. 1.
4. Stephen R. Covey, *The 7 Habits of Highly Effective Families*, New York: Golden Books, 1997, p. 77.
5. Laurie Beth Jones, *The Path: Creating Your Mission Statement for Work and for Life*, New York: Hyperion, 1996, pp. 33–70.

1 Looking for God's Best in All the Wrong Places

The clock is my dictator, I shall not rest.
It makes me lie down only when exhausted.
It leads me to deep depression, it hounds my soul.
It leads me in circles of frenzy for activity's sake.
Even though I run frantically from task to task,
I will never get it all done, for my "ideal" is with me.
Deadlines and my need for approval, they drive me.
They demand performance from me, beyond the limits of my schedule.
They anoint my head with migraines, my in-basket overflows.
Surely fatigue and time pressure shall follow me all the days of my life,
And I will dwell in the bonds of frustration forever.

Marcia K. Hornok, *Psalm 23, Antithesis*[1]

Going for the gold

Going for the Gold, Extreme Cool, High Status, I Want to be a Millionaire, A Mo Betta Life Man! Everyone is going for the gold. We are all racing along the freeway of life in our quest for the best. Where are we likely to find the good life for ourselves and those we care about? If the skyline of that land of milk and honey suddenly appeared over the next horizon would we even recognize it? Or could we be taken in by some very seductive, glittering counterfeits and take the wrong exit?

Finding the focus

We are convinced that deep down inside everyone wants the best God has for them. People are looking for the good life, which at its core includes wanting a satisfying way of life that counts for something. But the evidence suggests that most of us are missing the best and settling for less . . . often a lot less.

We are surrounded by many stories and competing visions of what constitutes the best . . . the good life and better future. The most prevalent story that fills our world today is a product of modern culture and our new global economy. The dream of the good life and better future at the centre of this story is a dream of economic growth, individual upscaling and ever expanding consumer choice that we call Boom City. And its dazzling skyline has become the most attractive dream for people all over the planet.

In this chapter we will argue that if we don't draft a mission statement that flows directly out of our faith, like Jesus did, then Boom City will define our mission statement for us. While many of us are constantly aware that the pressures we are under make our lives one long stress-race, we don't seem to understand where the pressure comes from. We seem to be largely unaware that many of us, including very sincere Christians, have allowed Boom City instead of our faith to define what's best for our lives and families. To the extent that we allow the dream that drives Boom City to define the direction and tempo for our lives and families; to that extent you can be sure we will miss the best that God has for us.

One reason numbers of us are beginning to question whether we are headed in the right direction is that we find ourselves trapped in the fast lane literally burning the rubber right off our tyres. A new contagion called "hurry sickness" is sweeping across the world. Hurry sickness is simply the consequence of people trying to jam more activity into 24 hours than is humanly possible . . . and becoming hyper-stressed in the process. Everywhere we work in Britain, Australia, New Zealand, Canada and the US, most people tell us they have to work harder and longer in this new global economy than even a few years ago.

As John Ortberg expressed in *The Life You've Always Wanted,* "One of the great delusions of our day is that hurrying will buy us more time."[2] Ortberg goes on to say "If we have hurry sickness, we are haunted by the fear that there are just not enough hours in the day to do what needs to be done. We will read faster, walk faster, talk faster, and when listening, nod faster to encourage the talker to accelerate. We will find ourselves chafing whenever we have to wait."[3] Hurry sickness is an epidemic sweeping across our world. It stresses our lives and leaves us exhausted and chronically guilty for all that we haven't done. Can you find some of your symptoms in this quick review of the afflicted?

Juggling with Julie in an on-line life

Julie is a 42-year-old mum who sees herself as a totally incompetent circus juggler. When she is home, her cell phone and beeper constantly interrupt meals and limit her family time. Each morning she staggers out of bed at 5 am in her London home so she can check her 65 e-mails before waking her two kids. She dashes out the door before they are off to school and races to the train. Her beeper goes off . . . reminding her that she should be home to take her oldest daughter to have braces fitted at 4 pm that day. But she won't be home until evening, so she grabs her cell phone to call her husband. Perhaps he can leave work early. But her cell phone is dead and she realizes she won't be able to call him until after he finishes with clients for the day. Julie sinks into her chair exhausted, feeling guilty because she has just dropped the ball yet again.

One reason people like Julie are so busy is that in the nineties the workplace changed dramatically. Now that we are all part of a new global economy, a growing number of us never leave work. In this new "hyperconnected" world many of us are on-line and on call 24 hours a day, 7 days a week, creating what has become known as a 24/7 lifestyle. Life has become a kind of extreme sport for many. The *New York Times* heralds, "Cell phones, pagers and wireless e-mail have created a workday that never ends. Whatever line people have drawn between work and leisure, between office and home is growing thinner than ever as a sense of obligation to stay connected to work all hours continues to grow."[4]

Sleepless in Cambridge with Matthew

Matthew is a 22-year-old student in a rush. He is in his final year at Cambridge and is anxious to complete his business degree so that he can start earning a six-figure income instead of "giving his money away" to the university. Matt seldom misses a lecture but is trying to restrict himself to four hours sleep a night so that he can run his small web-page business from 4 to 8 am before going to his 9 am class. He seems to be doing a better job than Julie of keeping all his balls in the air – except for one thing. In the last six months he has suffered increasingly from blackouts. He didn't worry when he occasionally blacked out in the library or even in class. But when he rolled his car on his way to Edinburgh last week it got his attention and he made an appointment for a checkup at the health clinic.

For Matthew and millions of other Westerners, stress, exhaustion and extreme busyness have become badges of distinction. "The frenetic sense of lost time and life out of control permeates our entire modern society."[5] Less than 67 per cent of adults in the US get 8 hours sleep. Some 43 per cent are so sleepy during the day that, like Matthew, they have serious problems functioning. Research reveals that we are getting a lot less sleep than we used to. Fifty-eight per cent of people surveyed said they suffered from insomnia at least a couple of nights a week, while 45 per cent said they would willingly sacrifice sleep to spend more time at work. Forty-three per cent said they were sacrificing sleep time to go on-line or watch TV, and 55 per cent of 18–29-year-olds confessed this is a chronic problem. One study showed 55 per cent of those under 25 involved in car crashes were suffering from sleep deprivation.[6]

Applause for Mark and Marjorie's busy life

Mark, a lawyer in Dallas, Texas, works 10 to 12 hours a day, often beginning at 5 or 6 am in order to have some time in the evenings for his family. But that time too is an incredible blur of activity as daughters who are challenged to be the best at everything are shuttled constantly from music lessons to soccer and basketball practice. On weekends Mark and his wife Marjorie dash to the mall to shop for the latest fashions then to the soccer field, to the basketball court and finally off to the local health club for their own weekly workout.

Marjorie and Mark are determined to model the "perfect Christian family". They live in a very upscale neighbourhood in Dallas and never like to miss church on Sunday. However this commitment is being eroded increasingly by the growing competition of Sunday morning soccer games for the kids. Marjorie often races into church ten or more minutes late and flops exhausted into the pew. She can rarely concentrate on the message and feels her spiritual life is slowly draining away. Mark is proud of his family's commitment to such a hectic schedule. He relishes the accolades of his friends and family, who constantly applaud his busy life while his entire family lives on the edge of exhaustion.

Mark and Marjorie, like too many of us, derive their sense of self-worth from outrageous busyness. "Stress has become a badge of honour of the millennium" stated Arlene Kagle, a psychologist who practises in Manhattan. "We lost the idea of the Sabbath as a day of rest long ago. Now we have lost evenings, nights and weekends as well . . . Then we complain – that is to say brag – that we're just so wound up and tense we can barely sleep . . ."[7] Sound familiar? Are you, your family or friends paying the high costs of your hurry sickness?

Diagnosing the cause of hurry sickness

Where does hurry sickness come from? Some people think it is simply a consequence of trying to crowd too much stuff into our already congested schedules. Of course that is part of it. Even those of us in Christian ministry can overdo it. In fact Christine wound up in the hospital in Tyler, Texas, in 1992 with Chronic Fatigue Syndrome as a consequence of trying to stretch herself too thinly while she was the Medical Director of

Mercy Ships. Christine knows first hand how Elijah felt in 1 Kings 19 when he exhausted himself working for God's cause. But she also used her exhaustion as a time to encounter God and find renewal and refocusing, like Elijah did at Mount Horeb.

Do you want to find out why so many of us struggle with chronic hurry sickness? Then check out how we have bought into someone else's notion of what is best. When we allow others to define what is important and of value for us, that in turn defines where we spend our time and money.

For example, in spite of their genuine faith, we believe Mark and Marjorie have unwittingly allowed Boom City to define what is best for their family. Their incredible busyness, which they wear like a badge of honour, is a direct result of their notion of the good life. Mark's drivenness can be traced back to the need to get to the top of the ladder in his law practice, even though it leaves very little time for his family and spiritual life. Marjorie and her daughters' drivenness can be traced directly back to the need to excel in all the suburban competitions from endless youth achievement projects to consumer competition in fashions, furnishings, vehicles and vacations. Given the unstated mission statements to which this family has unwittingly committed their lives it shouldn't be surprising that they are suffering from hurry sickness.

Welcome to Boom City

As we race along the crowded highway of our lives both sides of the road are congested with huge, electronic, three-dimensional billboards all promising the land of wine and roses in a place called Boom City. Whether we recognize it or not, most of us have embraced someone's notion, consciously or unconsciously, of what constitutes the good life and better future.

Hurry sickness begins here. Whatever vision we embrace as the good life and better future determines what is really

Off Ramp No. 1
Hurry sickness audit time

Are you struggling with hurry sickness? Are you exhausted? Is your high pressure timestyle taking a toll on your family life, relationships and spiritual life? Do you sense that you are missing the best that God has for you? Is it possible that one of the major reasons you are over-booked is that you too have allowed others to define your sense of what is important and of value?

We invite you to leave the fast lane and pull off to a quiet spot, get a notebook or journal and get to work. This book will be much more valuable to you if you participate in every "off ramp" exercise. Open your notebook and answer the following questions:

1. Outline where you spent your time during the past week and your money during the past month.

2. Where are you feeling the greatest pressure on your time schedule and your budget?

3. Where are you paying the highest costs from hurry sickness in your health, your relationships with family and friends, in your involvement in your church and relationship to God? How motivated are you to make some changes?

4. Hurry sickness audit time. Based on where you spent your time and money, what are the aspirations and values that seem to drive your life and where do they come from? Is your life driven by the expectations of your workplace, your suburban community, your family, friends and neighbours? Try setting your answer to music or put it in poetic verse and sing it or read it along with your other answers to your study group or to a friend.

important to us. What is important to us directly determines where we spend our time and money. So identifying our intended destinations gives us a shot at not only understanding why we are so crazily busy . . . but doing something about it.

It's tough on the frenetic motorway of life to decide which

off ramp to take to find our way home to the best God has for us. Some destinations are vivid and inviting, others lie on obscure and hidden back roads. Even people of serious faith all over the planet often have trouble discerning whether Boom City is really the city of hope or a land of illusions. To really understand what Boom City offers us we need to understand its earliest beginnings.

The storytellers of the Enlightenment told us a new story. They told us that if we co-operate with the laws governing the natural world all of society will automatically progress and life will get better and better. Construction of this gleaming metropolis actually began during the Enlightenment. Francis Bacon was one of its earliest architects. In his book, *The New Atlantis,* he sketched a vision of a technological paradise of affluence and unbelievable consumer choice. He assured us that this vision could be achieved through unleashing the power of science and technology to subdue the natural world and create a society of extraordinary comfort, security and wealth.

Essentially the storytellers of the Enlightenment took the vertical vision of the pursuit of the kingdom of God, that reigned during the Middle Ages, and tipped it on its side. Their focus became the horizontal vision of social progress, economic affluence and technological mastery. Today we call this dream the Western dream. This vision's notion of the good life is defined as getting ahead economically. It is a dream preoccupied exclusively with the here and now, focused on satisfying our needs for "more". This is the dream that both drives Boom City and makes it so attractive to many of us.

The industrial and cyber revolutions have made this gleaming city into a stunning reality. Boom City has emerged in modern society as much grander and more affluent than anything Bacon or those earliest architects ever imagined. Haven't you and your loved ones been enjoying life in this wonderland of "more"? Let's look at how Boom City is becoming an amazing global reality as we race into the 21st century.

In the nineties, as Tom explained in *Mustard Seed vs McWorld,* something altogether new happened to this city of affluence, technological innovation and incredible consumer choice . . . it went global. When the Berlin wall came down and the Soviet Union imploded all the centrally planned Marxist economies were thrown into the rubbish bin of history because they didn't work very well. Virtually every nation on earth joined the free-market race to the top. The United States has enjoyed an unprecedented ten-year economic boom. But the horrific terrorist attack of 11 September 2001 tipped us into a new global recession, and no one knows how long it will last or how much pain there will be.

What made possible the creation of this one-world economic order was the girding of the planet with a global electronic nervous system of satellite dishes, fax machines and the internet. Through this nervous system $1.5 trillion circulates around the earth every day.[8] As Dorothy said to Toto in *The Wizard of Oz,* "I don't think we are in Kansas anymore!" And we aren't in the 70s, 80s or 90s anymore either. We have moved into a new neighbourhood that offers incredible new affluence and ever-expanding consumer choice.

We visited the Seattle Home Show recently and caught a glimpse of this amazing new booming global economy. There were over 100 hot tub dealers. We wondered how Seattle, with a population of some one million occupants could support that many hot tub businesses. Then we remembered we live in Microsoft land where not only Bill Gates but hundreds of other new millionaires are building 20,000 to 40,000 square foot mansions . . . complete with four to six hot tubs plus lavish second homes also equipped with hot tubs. In the past decade we have seen the creation of more jobs and rising wages. Growing numbers of the poor have come off welfare and gone back to work.[9] The *New York Times* has heralded the economic boom as "the best of times".[10] And a host of articles in business magazines trumpet it simply doesn't get any better than this! Are you among those doing better?

As Boom City goes global, everywhere is beginning to look like everywhere else with all the same upscale shops, tourist accommodations and franchised fast food outlets. But Boom City is above all else a global 24/7 shopping mall . . . on-line all the time.[11] Internet shopping gives the consumer a remarkable opportunity to shop in the Boom City Mall for bargains literally from all over the world. One of the amazing aspects of this boom economy is that soon we will have the opportunity to design our own cars, furniture and wardrobes on-line. Many of us are experiencing a new unprecedented level of individual consumer choice.

In the creation of this new one-world economic order we have seen an absolute explosion of wealth for the top 20 per cent. More billionaires and millionaires were created in the past ten years than at any time in human history. Trump World Towers at United Nations Plaza in New York offers apartments with a panoramic view at the bargain basement prices of $13,400,000.[12] Builders can hardly keep up with the booming demand for yachts and the bigger the better. Titanic luxury at only $13 million.[13] Such a deal!

"I wanna be a gazillionaire geek"

Millionaire mania has gone global. Many countries now have some version of the explosively popular game show "Who wants to be a millionaire?".[14] In the United States an array of new shows continue to spin off. Some call it the "Millionaire effect". The motorways are congested with millions intent on crowding the wide off ramp headed towards this new Shangri-La of spectacular wealth and extravagant consumer choice.

"Why work for General Motors or anybody else when you can invent your own company, get rich and retire before you're 30?" Students at Massachusetts Institute of Technology's Sloan School of Business asked this question when 150 teams gathered for a unique competition to decide the best plan for new business start-ups. The contest is called "I Wanna Be a Gazillionaire Geek" and often those who win find venture capitalists ready to fund their start-ups. One of the recent winners was DirectHit, a web-research technology firm that helps users identify the most popular sites. This student project has actually attracted $1.5 million in investment as a new start-up.[15]

Of course not everyone wants to be a gazillionaire. Many people tell us they would be satisfied if they had just a little more money or a little more security than they have now. But when people do see a sudden increase in their income it is only a question of time before they are discontented again. While the scripture encourages us to be content in whatever situation we find ourselves the architects of Boom City are committed to persuading us to be chronically discontented.

Boosting for Boom City

So many people are doing well economically it's not hard to find boosters for Boom City. John Micklethwait and Adrian Wooldridge make a strong case in their book, *A Future Perfect*, that this new one-world economic order is indeed that much sought after El Dorado. They argue: "The simple fact is that globalization makes us richer – or makes enough of us richer to make the whole process worthwhile."[16] Are they right? Is the ultimate really defined in terms of economic freedom and individual choice? Is this new boom economy of rising affluence and ever-expanding consumer choice the real promised land or is it a land of illusions?

Hidden price tags for life in Boom City

"A very modern mood disorder has settled over the most prosperous nation there ever was. On the crest of the boom, there is sadness. In a time of peace, there is anxiety. Amidst unprecedented stimulation, there is boredom. Just what is going on? . . . The paradox can be lost on no one: America is enjoying unprecedented levels of prosperity, health care, life expectancy, food supply and peace. ('Things aren't just getting better,' as Sir John Tempelton put in his latest book, *Is Progress Speeding*

Up? Our Multiplying Multitudes of Blessings, 'they're getting better and better at a faster and faster rate.') Yet it's suffering unprecedented rates of depression."[17]

If the boosters of Boom City are right, and everything is "getting better and better at a faster and faster rate" why aren't we having a better time? Why are so many of us afflicted by hurry sickness, stress and depression? Without a doubt we do live in the most affluent period in human history where the greatest number are sharing in the bounty of a huge range of consumer delectables. But what the boosters of Boom City fail to mention is that there are some huge hidden price tags for life in this city of palatial wealth and incredible choice.

In our efforts to find the best many of us have been taken in by the extremely seductive advertisements along the freeway. Is the good life really all about getting a bigger piece of the rock and enjoying the delights of Boom City or is something else? Just what are the hidden price tags we are paying for the good life offered to us by the marketers of Boom City?

Price tag number one for the British middle class is plummeting savings rates and soaring bankruptcy. Apparently we are bingeing out of our savings and other people's money.

Tammy and Rob have been married for two years. They desperately want to settle down, start a family and take some time for short-term missions too. But they can't do either. Every penny goes to pay off student loans and enormous credit card debts Rob incurred before marriage. Rob explained, "I thought credit cards would take over where my parents left off. It really never occurred to me I would actually have to pay for my clothes, car and CDs. I naively thought I could go on borrowing money forever." Fortunately they have set a strict budget and they are beginning to climb out. But many others aren't as successful in turning their situation around.

Why are so many of us, like Rob, enjoying the bounty of Boom City in a way that threatens our very future? Answer: we have bought Boom City's message of discontent that we will never find the satisfaction we seek unless we keep on consuming whether we can afford it or not. How have we succumbed to this message that encourages us to be chronically discontented?

Until the early 1920s people only bought what they needed . . . the essentials of life – food to eat, clothes to wear and a roof over their heads. However, it was clear to business leaders of the day that if they simply sold people what they needed they wouldn't do much business so they created a fifth human need . . . the need for novelty. The marketers of Boom City convinced us that meeting our basic needs isn't enough . . . we must constantly be persuaded to buy the newest and the latest novelty to be successful human beings. Buchanan calls this addiction "The Cult of the Next Thing". "The Cult of the Next Thing proclaims, 'Crave and spend for the Kingdom of stuff is here'. It teaches that our lives are measured in the abundance of our possessions."[18]

In recent years these marketers have even convinced many of us that we are what we own and the more we own the more we are. They have actually persuaded us that our very identity and self-worth comes from the cars we drive, the neighbourhoods we live in and the brands we proudly wear. In fact we have become a society of unpaid walking advertisements for branded products. Incredibly there is a church in Phoenix, Arizona, that has even allowed itself to become branded with a corporate logo.

To make matters worse in this new global economy shareholders do not want 3 per cent to 5 per cent return on investment. They want 10 per cent, 15 per cent, or even 25 per cent if they can get it. The only way that is possible is for all of us, and particularly our kids, to consume at levels never seen before on this planet. We must constantly be convinced that yesterday's luxuries have become today's necessities. And the more we are persuaded to spend on our expensive lifestyles the more hours we will need to work which, as you will see, directly contributes to our hurry sickness . . . big time.

Long hours, conspicuous consumption

When we work with Christians in Britain, Canada, the United States, Australia and New Zealand we always ask the same question: "How many feel you are working harder and longer than a few years ago?" Invariably 70 per cent raise their hands. A report published by the TUC in 1999 showed that Britons work the longest hours in Europe – an average of 44 hours a week as compared to 39 in Holland, Belgium and Denmark and there is growing pressure on workers to work longer hours.[19] In 1977 less than half of families in Europe and North America relied on dual incomes. Today it has increased dramatically to two-thirds and is still climbing. Some women work simply to help pay the mounting bills and keep their families' heads above water. But growing numbers are working to satisfy our rapidly expanding appetites for more.[20]

In the US a new phenomenon is emerging, the four-income family. According to *Money Magazine* "Simply put it can now take four – or more – jobs to provide the level of comfort and financial security that one income delivered a few decades ago." As we have already seen growing numbers are a part of a new 24/7[21] labour force that never gets away from work. Do you find yourself or members of your family in this picture?

The message from Boom City is that our sense of identity, self-worth and purpose for life come not only from what we buy but also from where we work. Not only men but increasingly women seem to derive their greatest sense of purpose and personal identity from their jobs. Australian commentator Bob Santamaria declares that our new boom global economy has declared war on the family. He asserts that financial and work pressures of this highly demanding new economy are directly contributing to escalating family breakups.[22] Families need help here!

High price tags of Boom City for the young

The marketers of Boom City realized in the nineties that if they were to keep this boom economy booming they had to get all of us, but particularly the young, to consume at levels never seen before. In the documentary film *Affluenza*[23] we are shown a marketing executive training other marketing professionals. He challenges them, "You have to get kids branded by age 5 if you want to have their product loyalty for their entire lives." If you have ever tried to get a 5-year-old past McDonalds you know how successful they are. Gary Ruskin in an article in *Mothering* magazine exposes this effort by marketers to target our kids. He explains "If you own this child at an early age, you can own this child for years to come." [24] And both children and families are succumbing to this marketing pressure on the young to consume at levels never seen before. Have you experienced this pressure on the young?

Kids want more entertainment too. Reportedly the average American child is on-line 37 hours a week . . . TV, MTV, CDs, video games, internet chat rooms. And they are exposed to 3,000 to 4,000 advertisements a week. And that number is increasing as corporations invade both public and private schools with inexpensive curriculum that includes their corporate ads. "Advertising is a type of curriculum – the most pervasive in America today . . . They teach that the solutions to life's problems lie not in good values, hard work, or education, but in materialism and the purchasing of more and more things."[25] And we have seen evidence of this same phenomenon across the Western world from New Zealand to Norway.

Teenagers, too, are a major target for the branders of Boom City. Programmed to believe their very identity comes from being cool, they spend every waking minute trying to fit in, wear the right brands and portray the right image to their peers. "This was not a time for selling Tide and Snuggle to housewives", says Canadian activist Naomi Klein in speaking of the marketing strategies of the 1990s. "It was a time for beaming MTV, Nike, Hilfiger, Microsoft, Netscape and Wired to global teens and their overgrown imitators . . . Through this process, peer pressure emerged as a powerful market force, making the keeping-up-with-the Joneses consumerism of their suburban parents pale by comparison. As clothing retailer Elise Decoteau said of her teen shoppers, 'They run in packs. If you sell to one, you sell to everyone in their class and everyone in their school.'"[26] "Clique uniformity" and "social corralling" are the new reality for branded teens.[27]

Surprising numbers of parents are even caving in to their teens' demands for cosmetic surgery for everything from breast enlargement to liposuction.[28] The message of what's best in Boom City for all generations couldn't be clearer . . . it's all about individual gratification: "Got the urge?", "Is your mouth ready?", "Pamper yourself", "Seize the moment!", "Fortune smiles on you", "You deserve a break today!", "I will live my life on my terms!"

Extreme cool and high status

While conducting a church retreat in Olympia, Washington, we divided participants into two groups: those under 35 and those over 35. We asked the younger group to identify what is "extreme cool" in terms of where they shop, the brands they wear and what they drive. Their list included shopping at the Gap and Banana Republic, wearing cool brands like Tommy Hilfiger, Old Navy and Nike and driving cool cars like Jeeps, Jettas, and HUMVs. The over 35s had a little different idea of what constituted "high status": shopping at Nordstroms, brands like Ralph Lauren, Brooks Brothers and Calvin Klein, buying a waterfront home on the edge of Lake Washington in Bill Gates' neighbourhood, driving a Lexus, Saturn or SUV (Sports Utility Vehicle) with all the extras, and luxury cruise line vacations. Many of them expressed surprise at how important these items had become in their lives. One young woman candidly confessed that she needed to shop almost every day for clothes to be acceptable to her friends. Regardless of your income do you and your kids feel some of the pressure to achieve extreme cool and high status?

As we speed along the motorways of life there is a dawning realization for some that Boom City may not be the promised land and getting all the stuff may not be the good life after all. Many of us both inside and outside the church are discovering the land of affluence may indeed be a land of illusions. In the film *The Truman Show*, Christof, the producer of the imaginary world in which Truman lives, is asked why Truman has not discovered that his world is make-believe. He responds: "We accept the reality of the world with which we're presented." In another popular film, *The Matrix*, Morpheus describes the Matrix – the imaginary world in which human beings are living as "The world that has been pulled over your eyes to blind you from the truth." Have many of us, like the characters in these films, accepted Boom City's notion of reality and vision of the good life . . . no questions asked?

Of course most of us aren't living palatially. We are simply trying to make ends meet. But we still tend to buy into Boom City's notion of what constitutes happiness. Christian parents want what's best for their kids but too often we too, like those outside the faith, define what is best in terms of getting ahead economically. Are we simply the sum of the work we do and the things we buy or are we something more? Is happiness simply the sum of economic success for us and our kids or is it something more? Is it possible we are missing the best that God has for us?

David Myers, a psychologist at Hope College, asks "After four decades of rising affluence . . . are we happier . . . than before? We are not. Since 1957 the number of Americans who say they are 'very happy' has declined from 35 to 32 per cent. Meanwhile, the divorce rate has doubled, the teen suicide rate has nearly tripled . . . and more people than ever (particularly young adults) are depressed. I call this soaring wealth and shrinking spirit 'the American paradox'. More than ever we have big houses and broken homes, high incomes and low morale . . . In an age of plenty, we feel spiritual hunger."[29]

Branded for life

What has happened, we believe, is that we haven't just moved into Boom City, Boom City has moved into us. More than we recognize, Boom City has branded us and defined, even for people of vital faith, what is important and what is of value. We have unwittingly allowed Boom City to write the mission statement for our lives and families, but few of us seemed to notice. The Bible reminds us that "we are in the world but not of the world." We can't physically move out of this new booming consumer culture but we can move it out of us. We can reject the idolatry of acquisitiveness, covetousness and the pursuit of individual upscaling.

Paul outlines how all the followers of Jesus can get out of the fast lane and find God's best. ". . . I urge . . . in view of God's mercy, to offer your bodies as living sacrifices, holy and pleasing to God – this is your spiritual act of worship. Do not conform any longer to the pattern of this world, but be transformed by the renewing of your mind. Then you will be able to test and approve what God's will is – his good, pleasing and perfect will" (Romans 12:1–2). We will only find God's best when we refuse to conform any longer to the aspirations and values of Boom City and invite God to transform our inmost sense of what is important and of value which will in turn change the direction and tempo of our lives.

Boom City – finding your way out of town

Paul and Fiona Johnson found a way to move Boom City out of their lives and connect to a very different story and a very different view of what is best. At a seminar Christine held at Spring Harvest, she helped participants including Fiona and Paul to write a beginning biblical mission statement. The Johnsons returned home to Bristol and used their mission statement to reprioritize their entire lives. With a struggle they gave up some of the consumer addictions that were stressing out both their budget and their time schedule. They carved out daily time for scripture study and prayer where they had

Off Ramp No. 2
High status and extreme cool audit time

Come with us to another off ramp and bring your notebook or journal. Try to answer the following questions as candidly as possible:

1. If you are over 35, what is high status in your community . . . in terms of the most desirable places to live, the most prestigious jobs, the places to shop, the brands people wear, the vehicles they drive, the places they holiday, prestige kid activity and the premier schools for the young?

2. If you are under 35, what is extreme cool among people your age in terms of the brands they wear, the places they shop, the places they go, the cars they drive, the technology they use, the most prestigious jobs and the places they holiday?

3. Now get out your old magazines, scissors and glue and create a large collage of pictures, ads and words that playfully portray what is extreme cool or high status in your community.

4. High status, extreme cool audit time. To what extent do you honestly find your sense of what is best really comes from Boom City's notion of extreme cool and high status? Share your list, your pictorial montage and your candid confession of your struggle with your study group or a good friend . . . and pray to find God's best for your life.

very little time before. They set aside more weekly family time to enjoy their two kids. Fiona and Paul also set aside two hours a week to visit a local nursing home, where their kids read to the seniors. They began to discover, as many others have, that the good life of God is a life given away. The Johnsons also freed up more time for hospitality, treating their friends to food they love cooking from all over the world. Paul and Fiona tell us that they are enjoying the serious beginning they have made to find God's best for their lives and family.

If you want to join the Johnsons in finding a less stressed, more festive, way of life that counts for something, join us in the next chapter. We will discover in an ancient story and a future hope a new sense of purpose for our lives and loved ones. Remember when two disciples walked with Christ along the Emmaus road and they were so preoccupied that they didn't even recognize Jesus? Some of us are so preoccupied with our busy lives and the attractions of Boom City that we are missing both that personal encounter with God as well as the best that God has for us. Our God loves us very much and longs to set us free from our driven lives and help us find a way of life with a difference. That journey begins, as we will see, by rediscovering our place in God's story and with that a new compelling sense of direction for our lives.

Notes

1. *Discipleship Journal*, Issue 60, November/December 1990, p. 23.
2. John Ortberg, *The Life You've Always Wanted*, Grand Rapids: Zondervan Publishers, 1997, p. 82.
3. Ortberg, p. 84.
4. Katie Hafner, "For the Well Connected, All the World's an Office", *New York Times*, March 30, 2000, pp. D1 & D7.
5. Annetta Miller, "The Millennium Mind-Set: It's Here, It's Clear, Get Used to It", *American Demographics*, January 1999, p. 63.
6. Mary Harvey, "Sleepless in America", *American Demographics*, July 2000, pp. 9–10.
7. Joanne Kaufman, "What's the Best Thing About Stress? There's Plenty of It", *New York Times*, June 25, 2000, p. 4.
8. Tom Sine, *Mustard Seed vs McWorld: Reinventing Life and Faith for the Future*. (London: Monarch Books, 1999).
9. "Good Ble$$ America", *Christianity Today*, April 3, 2000, p. 34.

10. Peter D. Sutherland and John W. Sewell, "Gathering the Nations to Promote Globalization", New York Times, February 8, 1998, p. 1.
11. Kathleen Madigan and David Lindorff, "Consumers Have Money to Burn", Business Week, April 20, 1998, pp. 42–43.
12. Jerry Adler and Tara Weingarten, "Mansions Off the Rack", Newsweek, February 14, 2000, p. 60.
13. Craig Wilson, "Size Does Matter", USA Today, July 7, 2000, p. D1.
14. Barry Bearak, "Many, Many in India Want to Be a Millionaire", New York Times, August 30, 2000, p. 1.
15. Donna Foote, "Show Us the Money", Newsweek, April 19, 1999, pp. 43–45.
16. John Micklethwait and Adrian Wooldridge, A Future Perfect: The Challenge and Hidden Promise of Globalization, New York: Crown Business, 2000, p. 335.
17. Kalle Lasn and Bruce Grierson, "Malignant Sadness", Adbusters, June / July 2000, pp. 28–35.
18. Mark Buchanan, "The Cult of the Next Thing", The Covenant Companion, November 2000, p. 7.
19. BBC News Online: "Business: The Economy", August 26, 1999.
20. Tamar Lewin, "Men Assuming Bigger Share At Home New Survey Shows", New York Times, April 15, 1998, p. A16.
21. Lesley Alderman, "Here Comes the four-income family", Money Magazine, Feb 1995, p. 1. The term 24/7 is used as a metaphor for the modern lifestyle where people are often expected to be on call 24 hours a day, 7 days a week.
22. Bob Santamaria, "The Global Economy – At War with the Family", Humanity, July 1998, p. 6.
23. Affluenza, a documentary coproduced by KCTS/Seattle and Oregon Public Broadcasting 1997.
24. Gary Ruskin, "Why They Whine: How Corporations Prey on Children", Mothering magazine, Nov/Dec 1999, p. 42.

25. Ruskin, p. 43.
26. Naomi Klein, *No Logo*, Canada: Alfred A. Knopf Publishers, 2000, p. 68.
27. Adrian Nicole LeBlanc, "The Tyranny Of Cool", *New York Times* magazine, November 14, 1999, pp. 94–96.
28. Robert D. Putnam, *Bowling Alone: The Collapse and Renewal of American Community*, New York: Simon & Schuster, 2000, p. 260.
29. David G. Myers, "Wealth, Well-Being, and the New American Dream", *Enough: A Quarterly Report on Consumption, the Quality of Life and the Environment*, no. 12, Summer 2000, p. 5.

2 Looking for God's Best in an Ancient Story and a Future Hope

There is a day coming when the mountain of God's house
Will be The Mountain-solid, towering over all mountains. All nations
will . . . set out for it.
They'll say, "Come, let's climb God's mountain, go to the house of
Jacob.
He'll show us the way he works so we can live the way we are made."
Zion is the source of revelation. God's message comes from Jerusalem.
He'll settle things fairly between the nations . . .
They'll turn their swords into shovels, their spears into hoes.
No more will nation fight nation; they won't play war anymore.
Come let's live in light in the light of God.

Isaiah 2:1–4

The Message, by Eugene Peterson

"For I know the plans I have for you," declares the Lord,
"plans to prosper you and not to harm you,
plans to give you hope and a future."

Jeremiah 29:11

Who am I and what in the world am I here for?

One gloomy night, an ugly black creature with webbed feet and a long scaly tail emerged from the mud and slime at the bottom of a billabong (stream or creek) in the Australian outback. He wandered the countryside calling out plaintively to every animal that passed. "Who am I? Who am I?" he called to the wallaby and the emu. They looked him up and down and sniffed at his leathery hide. "You're horrible!" they exclaimed and bounded away. Then he met a platypus scurrying down to the water. "Who am I?" he called again. "You're a bunyip," the platypus proclaimed as he examined the huge webbed feet. But he didn't want to associate with the creature and swiftly swam away. Finally the bunyip met a scientist who looked right through him and said "You're a figment of my imagination, you don't really exist at all."

Lonely and depressed, the bunyip headed back to the billabong and sat sadly beside its peaceful waters. Suddenly something stirred again in the mud and slime at the bottom of the creek and another black shape emerged from the waters on the same quest for identity. "Who am I?" it cried plaintively. "You're a bunyip," cried the first creature smiling delightedly and with an affectionate hug added "and so am I."[1]

Finding the focus

Know the feeling? Have you ever wondered, like the bunyip, who you are and what you are on the planet for? In this postmodern age many people are struggling with the issues of both identity and purpose. It is the contention of this chapter that buying into the aspirations and values of the Boom City Mall will never provide a sense of identity or purpose that satisfies us. Our Creator God calls us to find both our sense of personal identity and life purpose from an ancient story and a resurrection hope.

If you are among those who are sick and tired of the stress-race, and if you are sincerely looking for God's best for your life you need look no further. In this chapter we will argue that as followers of Jesus Christ we will find God's best by heading for a new destination that has a very different character than Boom City. This new destination is called the City of Shalom. We will argue that the only way to find our way home to the City of Shalom is to do what Christ did . . . place God's purposes at the very centre of lives. If we make God's purposes our purposes we will finally find God's best . . . life with a difference.

Stephen Covey states that "the power of transcendent vision is greater than the power of the scripting deep inside the human personality and it subordinates it, submerges it, until the whole personality is reorganized in the accomplishment of that vision."[2] Where better to find a sense of a transcendent story than in an ancient faith, like Jeremiah did. He reminds us of a Creator, Deliverer God who offers us "a future and a hope".

One of the major reasons our faith often has so little impact on our sense of purpose is because it isn't really connected to that transcendent vision that is destined to transform a world. Too many of us have settled for a very small compartmental- ized faith that is seriously disconnected from our daily lives and God's hurting world. In this chapter, we will invite you to do some time travel to discover both how our faith has become dis- connected from life and enable you to reconnect to God's vision for a people and a world. On our first trip we journey back only 12 years and join Christine in Africa as she discovers the pos- sibilities of whole-life faith.

Discovering a whole-life faith in Africa

We arrive by way of time travel in a small village in Ghana. As a doctor Christine loves working in Africa. Laughing children follow us wherever we go and a warm open hospitality greets us at the door of every hut. What is most intriguing, however, is the deep spirituality that pervades the lives of these people. As the women plant their crops, we see them pray to the gods of the fields, as they draw water we see them pray to the gods of the river. We are told that even when someone is sick or there are broken relationships in the village, the elders recognize that spiritual forces are at work and they pray to the gods for reconciliation.

Christine says that initially the missionaries were excited whenever someone wanted to pray with them, thinking this meant they were attracted to Christianity. After a while they realized it didn't mean that at all. For the Africans, everything has a spiritual dimension and so needs a spiritual solution. Their animistic faith is the cohesive force holding their commu- nity together. Broken relationships between villagers, disas- trous harvests, and illness are all seen as symptoms of deeper spiritual problems. Christine was not attracted to their animistic deities, but she was attracted to their all-pervading faith and the possibility of a whole-life faith for her life too. She asked herself, "Is Christianity as all-encompassing of life as animism is?"

As we travel in Great Britain, the United States, Canada, Australia and New Zealand we find a growing hunger for spirituality particularly among the under 40s. But the spiritually hungry are looking for a vital whole-life faith, and seem to have little interest in what too many churches are offering . . . a 15-minute in the morning church on Sunday faith . . . in which Boom City too often determines both the direction and rhythm of our lives.

There is mounting evidence that in many churches we are settling for a compartmentalized Christianity that is largely disconnected from the rest of our lives. For example, Robert Wuthnow in *God and Mammon in America* states that there is virtually no connect between our Sunday morning faith and how we spend our money during the week.[3] As we saw in the last chapter many of us sincere Christians derive our life direction not from a transcendent faith but from the expectations of the places we work or the communities in which we live. Why does our faith seem to have so little influence in our daily lives?

Causes of a compartmentalized faith

One of the major reasons for our compartmentalized faith is that many of us have unwittingly bought into faith in a Jesus who only inhabits a small spiritual part of our lives. Somehow we haven't grasped that the Bible teaches Jesus is not just interested in a spiritual corner of our lives or in hanging out at church with us for a couple hours on Sunday. Jesus Christ is interested in seeing the gospel transform every part of our lives and every dimension of God's world. Jim Wallis helps explain our disconnect, "The gospel message has been molded to suit an increasingly narcissistic culture . . . modern conversion is about bringing

Jesus into our lives rather than bringing us into his . . . conversion is just for ourselves, not for the world. We ask how Jesus might fulfill our lives not how we might serve his kingdom."[4]

Another major reason for our compartmentalized faith is a dualistic world view in which many Christians see the spiritual realm, heaven, as divorced from the world in which we live. The widely held view that our final destination is a non-material heaven in the clouds directly contributes to a very spiritualized piety that has little to do with the rest of our lives. Tom Wright writes ". . . we hope to leave the earth and go off to 'heaven', in which . . . God's kingdom will be fully present and his will be perfectly done. All God's people will be there with him, and the earth will be left behind for ever." Wright goes on to point out that this ". . . very dualistic unJewish view has no claim to be Jesus' meaning when he teaches us to pray your kingdom come, your will be done on earth as it is in heaven".[5] ". . . The Creator intends to rescue the world not abolish it."[6] As we will see in the biblical vision God intends to make all things new including God's good creation and bring us home to a New Jerusalem . . . the City of Shalom.

Too often our spiritualized faith in this model is reduced to little more than a devotional lubricant to keep our gears from jamming as we race to get ahead in our careers or in our suburban communities. If you are serious about finding a direction for your life that flows directly from a whole-life faith then it is time to do a bit of diagnosis. Take the next off ramp to try and discover how much influence your Christian faith has on both your daily life and your sense of life focus.

Looking forward to the possibility of a whole-life faith

God *does* offer us a "future and a hope" but not just for us and our spiritual lives. God's future hope is about the transformation of every part of our lives and every facet of God's world. We aren't headed for the clouds. The scripture repeatedly

Off Ramp No. 3

Finding the disconnect

In your journal, answer the following questions as candidly as possible:
1. Sample three Christian friends and ask them to describe
their view of heaven and compare it with your own. Do you find
your view of heaven and that of your friends is in the clouds and
largely divorced from this world?
2. How much time did you spend in worship and in your private
devotional life last week?
3. How many decisions that you made last week regarding how
you used time or money were directly influenced by your faith or
by biblical principles?
4. Is there a disconnect between your spiritual faith and the overall
direction of your life? Draw a picture that portrays how your faith
is influencing both the direction of your life and your stewardship
of time and money. Share your picture with your group or with a
friend and prayerfully explore how you can find your way to live a
fuller, more whole-life faith that has more influence on your entire
life.

affirms that God plans to make all things new, including the
creation. God is going to create a new heaven and a new earth
in which we will be welcomed home as a community of resurrected persons with all those who have gone before us to a new
Jerusalem of celebration and restoration. Jesus didn't come to
offer us a little private piety to work in around our busy lives
but offered a new reason for being . . . to join him in seeing his
new order bring that welcomed celebration and restoration into
the lives of others. God's great restoration project begins with
the word *shalom*.

At the very centre of God's dream for a people and a world
is the biblical word *shalom*. Richard Foster reminds us in
Freedom of Simplicity that "This wonderful vision of *shalom*

begins and ends our Bible. In the creation story God brought order and harmony out of chaos. In the Revelation of John we look forward to the glorious wholeness of a new heaven and a new earth."[7] Foster adds, "From the disruption of *shalom* in the Garden of Eden to its total renewal in the new Jerusalem, the object of all of God's work is the recovery of *shalom* in his creation."[8]

The original meaning is far more than the usual English translation "peace". "Wholeness" or "completeness"[9] are better, but even these words are inadequate. In essence *shalom* embraces God's desire to restore all things to the wholeness and harmony of relationship in which they were originally created. It is no wonder the children of Israel greeted each other with the word *shalom*. It was really an expression of God's mission statement for them. A Jewish friend told Christine that originally this greeting meant "May you live in anticipation of the day when God makes all things whole again." We are calling that destination the City of Shalom.

Introducing the Prince of Shalom

The coming of the Messiah of God didn't just have to do with God bringing wholeness to a small spiritual compartment of our lives, but to every part of our lives and God's world including those suffering from oppression and warfare. Listen again to Isaiah's vision of the coming of the Prince of Shalom and the scope of wholeness that God intends. "The people who walked in darkness have seen a great light. For those who lived in the land of deep shadows – light! sunbursts of light! You repopulated the nation, you expanded its joy. Oh, they're so glad in your presence! Festival joy! The joy of a great celebration, sharing rich gifts and warm greetings. The abuse of oppressors, the cruelty of tyrants – all their whips and cudgels and curses – is gone, done away with, a deliverance as surprising and sudden as Gideon's victory over Midian. The boots of all invading troops, along with shirts soaked in innocent blood, will be piled up in a heap and burned, a fire that will burn for days! For a child has been born – for us! The gift of a son for us! He'll take over the running of the world. His names will be Amazing Counselor, Strong God, Eternal Father, Prince of Wholeness [Shalom]. His ruling authority will grow, and there'll be no limits to the wholeness (Shalom) he brings. He rules from David's historic throne over that promised kingdom. He'll put that kingdom on firm footing and keep it going with fair dealing and right living, beginning now and lasting always. The Zeal of God . . . will do all this" (Isaiah 9:2–7).

If we want to find both a purpose for our lives and a basis for a whole-life faith then we need to ask: "What is God on about?" We need to go back to the Bible and try to understand God's end game . . . God's shalom purposes for the human future and the created order. Jesus was absolutely captured by God's vision of a new shalom order that isn't located in the clouds but is destined to make all things new in the world which we know.

Jesus living on purpose

Let's take our next time travel trip back to first-century Israel. This time we land right in the middle of a dusty street in a small town. As we move through a throng of people and sheep we begin to remember. We remember that waves of colonizing forces from Greece and Rome have forever changed the culture of Jewish society. We remember that the Jews no longer speak Hebrew, in which their sacred books are written. Instead they have adopted the common Aramaic of the eastern provinces of the Roman Empire. We remember how their lives must have been filled with a sense of despair and futility. Thomas Cahill asks "What does it take for a whole people to give up their language, their mother tongue? Does it mean that their common hopes and dreams have already been shattered?"[10] In such a world in which ancient faith and future hope has seemingly been trampled under the wheels of trade, commerce and galling Roman occupation it must have been very difficult to believe their God would ever intervene in a way that would offer this people "a future and a hope".

We follow the small group of people as they walk down a narrow winding street of this Galilean village. In fact we follow them through an archway into a large hall. As the crowd hushes a young man stands up, unrolls a scroll from the prophet Isaiah and reads the following words with authority, "'The Spirit of the Lord is on me, because he has anointed me to preach good news to the poor. He has sent me to proclaim freedom for the prisoners and recovery of sight for the blind, to release the oppressed, to proclaim the year of the Lord's favor.' Then he rolled up the scroll, gave it back to the attendant and sat down. The eyes of everyone in the synagogue were fastened on him, and he began by saying to them, 'Today this scripture is fulfilled in your hearing'" (Luke 4:18–21).

This must have been a startling moment for all who were there. After centuries of silence in which the occupying powers seemed to define the ultimate reality, like Boom City does for us today, these people hear a prophetic voice. Jesus reminded his listeners that the creator God is not out to lunch but is still calling the shots. He reminded them not only that their God is alive and well but that this God has shalom purposes for their lives and for the entire world that look very different from the culture in which they find themselves.

Perhaps the most startling aspect of Jesus' announcement to this hometown audience was that he intended to make the purposes of God of Israel his own purposes . . . "to preach good news to the poor . . . to proclaim freedom for the prisoners and recovery of sight to the blind, to release the oppressed, to proclaim the year of the Lord's favor." In other words, Jesus was not content to allow the dominant culture of his time to determine the direction of his life. Instead Jesus intentionally used the scripture that described God's shalom purposes to define a mission statement for his own life. To follow this Jesus and find God's best for our lives we need to do the same thing that Jesus did and make God's purposes our purposes.

One cannot read the gospels without being impressed at both the whole-life character of his faith and how single-mindedly Jesus devoted his life to seeing God's kingdom come on earth as it is in heaven. In Jesus Christ God's loving purposes for a people and a world have literally broken into our midst. Jesus not only proclaimed the good news of the kingdom, he demonstrated it. Every time he healed the sick, fed the hungry, hugged kids and brought good news to the poor we are shown glimpses of God's shalom kingdom . . . a preview of coming attractions.

Jesus and his friends . . . a glimpse of a new family and a new future

Jesus formed a small motley community, a new family, that also became something of a living, breathing foretaste of the shalom community envisioned by the prophets. Those first disciples were not involved in a 15-minute encounter in the morning house church on the Sabbath faith in which the dominant culture still dictated the terms of their lives. Those first disciples *got it*. They understood that to be disciples of Jesus meant committing their lives not only to God but also to the shalom purposes of God. Just like Jesus they too made God's purposes their purposes and found the best that God had for them . . . a whole-life faith that was more about giving than getting.

Richard Middleton and Bryan Walsh state that Jesus came rejecting "the world of grasping" that characterized his age and ours "and affirms 'the world of the gift'. He comes as an agent of the kingdom of God, dispensing gifts of the kingdom to those who are dispossessed. His ministry of healing exorcism, table fellowship and teaching restored the broken, freed the oppressed, welcomed the outcast and taught a new path way home."[11] Jesus comes to us not only as living proof that God's future has broken into our world but as a living disclosure of a God that promises to make all things new.

"In Jesus himself" Tom Wright observes, "we see the biblical portrait of YHWH come to life; the loving God rolling up his sleeves (Isaiah 52:10) to do in his person the job that no one else could do; the creator God giving new life; the God who works *through* his created world and supremely through his human creatures; the faithful God dwelling in the midst of his people; the stern, tender God, relentlessly opposed to all that destroys or distorts the good creation and especially human beings, but recklessly loving all those in need or distress . . . It is an Old Testament YHWH but it fits Jesus like a glove."[12]

An instrument of torture: an agent of transformation

What sets Christianity apart from all other world religions is that we serve a crucified God. We serve a God who knows first hand the squalor of a refugee camp, the terror of death squads and the brutality of a criminal's execution. "The cross is the surest, truest and deepest window on the very heart and character of the living and loving God."[13] It is through the cross that all that would defeat and destroy the work of God is destroyed. It is through the cross that God intends to redeem a people and transform a world. It is through the cross that God will finally bring us home to a world made new.

South African missiologist David Bosch tells us that "there is, in Jesus' ministry, no tension between saving from sin and saving from physical ailment, between the spiritual and the social."[14] Salvation carries with it the same sense of transformation that comes with God's promise to restore all things to wholeness. As Paul affirms "For God was pleased to have all His fullness dwell in Him [Christ], and through Him to reconcile to Himself *all things*, whether things on earth or things in heaven, by making peace through His blood, shed on the cross" (Colossians 1:19, 20). Not only are we reconciled to God through Christ's brutal death on the cross, but all things are reconciled "through his blood".[15]

Finally, it is through the resurrection of Christ that we know God's promised future will fully break into our world and

God's purposes will be fully realized. Peter reminds us that we have been born into a living hope "through the resurrection of Jesus Christ from the dead" (1 Peter 1:3). Even as Christ rose from the dead, 1 Corinthians assures us, we will also rise not as spirits but as whole persons coming home together to the shalom future of God.

When we were in Rome several years ago, we visited the Vatican Museum. Down in a quiet room in the basement we made a wonderful discovery. Here stood a huge collection of sarcophagal art from the first through third centuries. Unlike the often sombre and depressing medieval art which focused on themes like the temptation and suffering of Christ, the sarcophagal art presented images of the shalom of God. Here chiselled in stone coffins of long-forgotten people of faith are the most exciting images of celebration and hope we have ever seen. Christ riding on a donkey making his triumphal entry into Jerusalem heralding the coming of God's kingdom was a central theme. Swirling around Jesus were throngs of people joyously waving palm branches. Some who had been healed carried their beds above their heads, hungry people were being fed with fish and bread, and numbers of believers were pictured standing up on their caskets with their arms in the air welcoming the resurrection of God's new future.

Remember that the central message Jesus came proclaiming was, "Good news! Good news the future of God has broken into our midst!" "The time has come . . . the kingdom of God is near . . ." (Mark 1:15). The only way we can fully understand this good news that Jesus preached and that he and that first community demonstrated is to take some trips back to our ancient Jewish past to understand what God's shalom purposes were for a people and a world.

God's shalom project offers us a purpose and hope

"In the beginning God." Out of nothing God created everything. Jurgen Moltmann suggested that creation is aligned toward the future because God had a clear sense of purpose for the entire creation.[16] Even after the Fall God didn't give up on us. Scripture tells us that God's intention from the beginning was to create a new people, a new community that was to be a foreshadowing of the new transformed future that we are calling the City of Shalom.

The Jews were very aware that God created the world to live in *shalom* – in peaceful and loving, caring relationships. They knew the Fall destroyed this harmony. It fractured the spirit of togetherness that bound us to God, each other and God's wonderful creation. Instead of mutual love and harmony of the world God created, the Fall isolated each of us into our own private worlds of self-centredness, self-interest and greed. God's shalom project was not to simply reverse the damage done at the Fall but to create a new community knit together in love and harmony . . . a foretaste of the future.

Walter Brueggemann, in his important book *Living Toward a Vision: Biblical Reflections on Shalom*, declares, "*Shalom* is a creation time when all God's creation eases up on hostility and destruction and finds another way of relating. No wonder creation culminates in the peace and joy of Sabbath (Genesis 2:1–4) when all lie down and none make us afraid."[17] The shalom purposes of God were intended to transform not only our relationship to God, but also our relationships to one another and to God's good creation. The Israelites were called to create a pilot project in which they would be different from the people around them, not only religiously and morally, but relationally, economically and politically too. They weren't called to a narrow piety but to a whole-life faith that was intended to transform every part of their lives and society.

In search of the promised land

Let's travel back again to an ancient past to try to understand what Yahweh had in mind for our human future. On our trip back to the dawn of human history we land in the ancient land

of Sumer. Travelling back ". . . like characters in a Steven
Spielberg film we would find . . . human life, seen as a pale re-
enactment of the life of the eternal heavens . . . ruled by a fate
beyond the pitiful limited powers of human beings . . . one's fate
was written in the clouds and could not be changed."[18] wrote
Thomas Cahill. The Sumerians, like most ancient people, lived
a fatalistic existence lashed on the blind wheel of birth and
death. They were pawns of the gods without any sense of
purpose for human existence.

As we arrive we meet two aged residents of Sumer who had
an unexpected encounter with a God of the high places who
was very different from the deities of the Sumerians. In fact this
God of the high places offered them a future and hope. Not just
for themselves and their offspring but for all humankind. This
was not just a startlingly new concept. This view of a God with
a mission was incredibly revolutionary both then and now.[19]
This God of the high places was a God of surprises promising
to bless the human future through the offspring of an aged,
childless couple. Sarah laughed at this preposterous proposal
but it wasn't long until her laughter was drowned out by the
cries of her first-born child. Abraham and Sarah learned to
take this God very seriously. As you know they packed up their
huge extended family and set out for the land and the future
God had promised them (Genesis 12:1–5). As the author of
Hebrews reminds us ". . . he [Abraham] was looking forward to
the city with foundations, whose architect and builder is God"
(Hebrews 11:10). This is really how God's new story began.

Travelling ahead several hundred years we find ourselves not
in the land flowing with milk and honey but in a miserable, des-
olate wasteland. Here we meet Moses leading a huge group of
former Hebrew slaves out of Egypt in search of the same land
promised to Abraham and Sarah. God reminds them, "If you
follow my decrees and are careful to obey my commands, I will
send you rain in its season, and the ground will yield its crops
and the trees of the field their fruit . . . you will eat all the food
you want and live in safety in your land. I will grant *shalom* in

the land and you will lie down and no one will make you afraid (Leviticus 26:3–6). And God make it clear that no one will be allowed to enjoy the shalom of God until every family had been able to find their own place in which to settle in this new homeland.

Building the City of Shalom

In the ten commandments Yahweh instituted a new relationship to this chosen people in which they were to swear singular fidelity to the God who had liberated them from their grinding slavery. The decalogue raised a high new ethical standard for their relationships to others as well. This band of former slaves were called to be set apart dramatically from their neighbours in their worship of Yahweh and in their responsible, caring relationships to one another. But the Architect of this new shalom community intended that those transformed relationships would alter their politics and economics too. For example, God instituted Sabbath and Jubilee principles to ensure that this new shalom community was distinguished from its neighbours by how it cared for its poorest members. Provision was to be made for the widow, orphan and immigrant. Jubilee was instituted so that poverty would not become a crippling reality for those at the margins as it was in other cultures.

Every 50 years debts were to be forgiven and slaves set free so that the curse of generational poverty could be broken and the offspring of the poor given a fresh start. Doug Meeks states that "The egalitarian impetus of God's economy is against all forms of domination by which the powerful 'grinds the faces of the poor' . . . It does not mean a conformist or a leveled society." But it does mean they were to become a part of a new shalom household where the poor were set free from grinding poverty.[20]

While their neighbours all had a political system in which a king and a privileged elite ruled the impoverished masses, the children of Israel were to be ruled by their God. Initially Israel followed this model. And archeological evidence shows that they were a fairly egalitarian society in which all houses were roughly the same size. There wasn't the huge disparity between rich and poor that characterized surrounding nations.

Eviction notice from the city

Tragically, even before the construction of the City of Shalom was complete the inhabitants earned themselves an eviction notice. They constantly found ways to provoke and disappoint the God who had mercy on them. Somehow they must have thought that the Architect of this project wasn't serious about creating a new community based on very different values from those of their neighbours. Part of the problems began when these residents decided they wanted to have a king just like everyone else. So God tried to be flexible and gave them a king.

But it wasn't long before it became clear why God thought this was a bad idea. Starting with King Solomon, Israel's kings quickly moved away from many of the key principles of the City of Shalom and began to seriously compromise God's project. Solomon brought the gods of his foreign wives into Yahweh's new community. The ruling class became greedy and began accumulating power and wealth for themselves. Solomon even enslaved his own people (1 Kings 9:15, 20–22) in order to build a palatial palace for himself. Like other nations Israel developed a wealthy ruling class who enjoyed their lavish lifestyles at the expense of their poor neighbours. Peace no longer depended on their covenant with God but on their military might and their intertribal marriages . . . just like all the other nations.

Into this environment the prophets came to the rulers with a scalding message of judgment for substituting their self-interested agendas for the shalom purposes of God. God brought judgment upon them for their idolatry, sexual immorality and their prospering at the expense of their poorest neighbours. The prophet Jeremiah declared "From the least to the greatest, all are greedy for gain; prophets and priests alike, all practice deceit. They dress the wound of my people as though it were not serious. 'Peace, peace' they say, when there is no peace"(Jeremiah 6: 13–14). Unfortunately, the self-interested agendas that brought Israel down, being "greedy for gain", aren't any different from the greed and covetousness that keeps Boom City booming today.

God did punish the Jews by allowing Babylon to invade Israel, destroy Jerusalem and take them into a galling captivity. There is an amazing 160-year interlude between Isaiah 39, in which the prophet Isaiah announces the coming captivity, and Isaiah 40 when God announces that their captivity is ended . . . God brought them back home to Jerusalem "authorizing a superhighway across the desert between Babylon and Jerusalem for an easy, triumphant, dazzling return home",[21] declares Walter Brueggemann. "A voice cries out: 'In the wilderness prepare the way of the Lord, make straight in the desert a highway for our God. Every valley shall be lifted up, and every mountain and hill shall be made low; the uneven ground shall become level and the rough places a plain. Then the glory of the Lord shall be revealed and all nations will see it together, and the mouth of the Lord has spoken'" (Isaiah 40: 3–5). We are reminded in Mary's Magnificat that the high places of arrogance will indeed be pulled down and the humble, and the poor will be lifted up and brought home on the super highway of God.

Back to the future . . . discovering the shalom vision for all peoples

Now that we have travelled back to the past to be reminded of God's intention to create a new shalom community, let's travel back to the future to see how the Creator God plans to end this remarkable drama. In the writings of the prophets we are invited to enter the future to see what the Author has in mind for a people and a world. God's shalom purposes have not changed since the first act of this drama. They have only become richer and more compelling as the prophets paint with vivid colours and compelling hope.

Somehow the prophets use the ancient imagery of the Jews coming home from captivity in Babylon to paint a richly variegated picture of a people and a world made new. It is a picture of a day in which all of God's children will come home to the shalom future of God. The prophets flash forward to a day when all of us who have chosen to follow God will join the great parade of those coming home down a super highway to a transformed Zion and Jerusalem. The good news is we don't have to wait to take the off ramp onto God's super highway. We can discover the best that God has for us right now. If we can understand God's purposes for the human future then we can make those purposes our purposes today. Keep a list of the purposes of God as we time travel forward into the new future and the hope God has for a people and a world.

Coming home to a new Jerusalem

As we travel into the future picture yourself on God's new highway joining a huge throng from many different nations and cultures who are singing and dancing as we come home to God's best in the City of Shalom. "There is a day coming when the mountain of God's House will be The Mountain- solid towering over all mountains . . . all nations will set out for it. They'll say 'Come, let's climb God's Mountain, go to the House of the God of Jacob. He'll show us the way he works so we can live the way we are made.' Zion's the source of revelation. God's message comes from Jerusalem. He'll settle things fairly between nations. He'll make things right between many peoples. They'll turn their swords into shovels, their spears into hoes. No more will nation fight nation; they won't play war anymore. Come, family of Jacob, let's live in the light of God" (Isaiah 2: 2–5). God's shalom purposes clearly include being reconciled not only to God but to one another. God intends a homecoming day in which we will no longer settle our differences by conflict and violence. The great homecoming of God will also be a tremendous time of feasting and celebrating. Listen to the imagery of the homecoming celebration in Isaiah 25: 6–10.

"But here on this mountain, God . . . will throw a feast for all the people of the world, a feast of the finest foods, a feast of vintage wines, a feast of seven courses, a feast of lavish gourmet desserts. And here on this mountain, God will banish the pall of doom hanging over all peoples . . . Yes, he will banish death forever. And God will wipe the tears from every face. . . . Yes, God says so! Also at that time, people will say, 'Look at what has happened! This is our God! We waited for him and he showed up to save us! This God, the one we waited for! Let's celebrate, sing the joys of his salvation. God's hand rests on this mountain!' (Isaiah 25: 6–10).

In Isaiah 35: 1–7 we see that the physically disabled will dance down the highway, the blind will see this incredible pageant and the deaf will hear the jubilant singing in many different tongues. In this passage we see that the Creator God not only intends to bring healing to the disabled but even restoration to God's beautiful creation. Ezekiel and Isaiah both speak of *a covenant of shalom* and of a time when God will bring the straying ones back home again. "I will make a covenant of shalom with them . . . I will bless them and the places surrounding my hill. I will send down showers in season . . . The trees of the field will yield their fruit and the ground will yield its crops; the people will be secure in their land. They will know I am the Lord when I break the bars of their yoke and rescue them from the hands of those who enslaved them" Ezekiel 34:25–27. God invites us to come home to a new future as a resurrected community set free by our God.

The City of Shalom is not just about God's covenant with us. It really is a new destination for the human future. We aren't headed to the clouds. As we have seen, the Bible teaches that at the return of Christ we will come home as a great resurrected community of people from every tribe and culture to a new heaven and a new earth. Together we will climb a new mountain and be welcomed into a new city. As we climb that mountain we are told that the blind will see, the deaf will hear and the disabled will race to the top. Justice will come to the poor and the instruments of war will be transformed into the implements of peace. The God of all shalom will welcome us home to a lavish banquet where we will be reunited with loved ones and family that we have never known . . . and we will shout our thanks to the One who brought us home to the City of Shalom.

Visions of the City of Shalom

When we work with college students we often share some of these powerful biblical images of the great homecoming of God. Then we break the students into three groups. We have one group draw a picture of the Great Homecoming. A second group is invited to plan a party that captures the spirit of the homecoming. And the third group is asked to write a song. Typically the first group draws a vibrant picture celebration with people from many different cultures and colours going up the mountain of God together . . . arm in arm. Wheelchairs and crutches are abandoned along the way. At the top of the mountain feasting and jubilation is the focal point and the poor are the guests of honour as the reign of God is announced.

At one college in Chicago a group of students envisioned taking over a city park near the lakefront over a weekend to give Chicago residents a taste of God's kingdom. They planned a party in which African-American, Latino, Asian and Anglo churches would be invited to bring food, dance and music to the park and put on an event celebrating the end of violence and injustice and proclaiming our oneness as the new shalom family of God. When we worked with Mennonite youth workers in Winnipeg, Canada, they came up with words to a rousing song about the great homecoming of God. The words are: "A feast of food and finest wine . . . Yahweh calls us come and dine. Shatter the yoke, break the rod, plunge into the shalom of

God!" At the end of class they serpentined through the denominational offices of the Mennonite Church singing the song and
joyously disrupting everyone's work as they joined in the jubilation.

Boom City vs shalom

Let's briefly contrast the shalom purposes of God for a people
and a world with those that power Boom City. First, let us make
it clear that there are many benefits we receive from the new
economic order in which we live. Second, we aren't suggesting
that we try to physically move out of modern culture. But we
are urging that we move Boom City out of us. In other words
we are suggesting that we no longer allow the aspirations that
power Boom City to define the mission statements of our lives.
Instead we are urging that we all find a new sense of purpose
for our lives that flows directly out of the shalom purposes of
God. How are the aspirations of Boom City different from
those that motivate the City of Shalom?

The architects of Boom City want us to succumb to the
fiction that we will find the best by focusing on our own lives
and seeking to satisfy our own needs. They have attempted to
make all the seven deadly sins, including greed and covetousness, the new virtues of this new global economy. The only one
that didn't make the list was, of course, sloth. As we have seen,
the purposes of Boom City are to elevate the individual pursuit
of happiness as the cardinal goal of life. It is about extreme cool
and achieving high status. Getting ahead in the workplace, individual economic upscaling and ever-expanding consumer
choice constitute the true definition of the good life. Are you
ready to accept the message that both our life purpose and our
identity come primarily through economic achievement? Or is
there something more? I suspect deep down we all know the rat
race is a fraud. It never was the good life and we all recognize
the high costs we have paid in our health, our personal relationships and our spiritual lives for a bogus dream.

The City of Shalom provides a vision for the future that isn't all about me. It is about a world that God loves and Christ died for. It is about a creator God who purposes to redeem a people and transform a world. It is about the shalom promise of the personal wholeness we all crave and ultimately experience by being reconciled to God through the cross of Jesus Christ. While of course we encounter God personally, we will only be redeemed as a great community. And we only find the wholeness we seek as we work for the wholeness in our entire family of faith.

The shalom purposes of God are not about the individual pursuit of happiness. Jesus couldn't have been clearer. The good life of God is found not in seeking life but paradoxically through losing our lives in service to others. As followers of Christ we are called to do what he did . . . to put the shalom purposes of God, not the addictions and idolatries of modern culture, at the centre of our lives and our communities of faith. As we have seen, the shalom purposes of God are to bring wholeness to every part of God's world.

The Bible tells us over and over that God intends to make all things new . . . not just the spiritual realm, but all of human life and experience. When we come home as a great resurrected community to the great homecoming God intends we will enter a celebrative future in which the blind see, the deaf hear and the lame dance for joy. It is a future in which justice comes for the poor, peace to the nations and all divisions of race, culture and national identity disappear as we discover we are all family together and we worship our God forever. The power of self-interest, greed and violence will be destroyed as the lamb and the lion lay down together and we live in the City of Shalom forever.

Doesn't this vision of the shalom future of God have at its core a very different notion of the good life and a better future? While it cares very personally for the individual it isn't individualistic. While it embraces the material world it isn't materialistic. While it is centred in celebration it isn't hedonistic. It is a vision that cares much more about making a difference than making a dollar. It is about seeing the lives of real people

Off Ramp No. 4
Picturing coming home to God's best

 Take your journal and your Bible and find a quiet place and if possible at least an hour or two for this important time of reflection on the shalom purposes of God.

1. Read back over the biblical imagery of the shalom vision of God in this chapter and in the biblical references cited. Meditate on these images and reflect on how they are different from the seductive messages of our modern culture. Write down where you still find yourself in terms of the competing aspirations of Boom City and the City of Shalom.

2. Reflect on those areas of human need that touch you most deeply in the lives of people in your church, your community and the larger world . . . from neglected seniors and teens destroying their lives with drugs to AIDS orphans in Africa and young people in Europe desperately trying to find a basis for faith. Now stop and imagine the shalom of God flooding into that situation and bringing God's loving transformation, and write it down.

3. Now imagine how the direction and the character of your life might change if you did what Jesus and many other disciples have done . . . to place the shalom purposes of God at the centre of your life.

4. Finally try drawing a picture of how the coming of the shalom of God might transform both your life and those areas of need that most urgently touch your heart and share all you have written and drawn with your group or with a friend . . . praying earnestly that "God's kingdom will come and God's will be done on earth as it is in heaven!"

changed by the power of God. It is an amazing opportunity to discover how the Living God can use our mustard seeds to make a little difference in our hurting world. It is an invitation to find God's best . . . a way of life that counts.

Do you sincerely want the best that God has for you? Let's take the off ramp and examine which purposes we want to place at the centre of our lives.

Where do we begin?

Every follower of Jesus Christ needs to begin where he and those first disciples began. We need to commit our lives not only to God but to the shalom purposes of God . . . "sight for the blind, release to the captives and good news to the poor." We are called to make God's purposes our purposes and Christ's vocation our vocation. Then and only then can we begin to improvise our stories within The Story. In the next chapter we invite you to work directly from a sense of God's shalom purposes to actually write a beginning mission statement for your life to discover the possibilities of *living on purpose*.

Notes

1. The bunyip is an intriguing Australian animal that originated in the myths of the aboriginal dreamtime. It has been immortalized in Christine's favourite Australian children's story by Jenny Wagner & Ron Brooks, *The Bunyip of Berkeley's Creek*, Sydney: Puffin Books, 1974.

2. Stephen R. Covey, A. Roger Merrill and Rebecca R. Merrill, *First Things First*, New York: Simon & Schuster, 1994, p. 106.

3. Robert Wuthnow, *God and Mammon in America*, New York: Macmillan, 1994, pp. 150–151.

4. Jim Wallis, *The Call to Conversion: Recovering the Gospel for These Times*, San Francisco: Harper & Row, 1981, p. 28.

5. Tom Wright, *The Myth of the Millennium*, London: Azure (SPCK), 1999, pp. 15–16.

6. Wright, p. 19.

7. Richard J. Foster, *Freedom of Simplicity*, San Francisco: Harper Collins, 1984, p. 30.

8. James E. Metzler, "Shalom is the Mission", *Mission and Peace Witness* (Scottsdale, Arizona Herald Press, 1978), p. 40.

9. For a comprehensive discussion of shalom see *Living*

Towards a Vision: Biblical Reflections on Shalom, Walter Brueggemann, New York: United Church Press, 1976.

10. Thomas Cahill, *Desire of the Everlasting Hills*, New York: Anchor Books, 1999, p. 57.

11. J. Richard Middleton and Bryan J. Walsh, *Truth is Stranger Than it Used to Be: Biblical Faith in a Postmodern Age*, Downers Grove: InterVarsity Press, 1995, p. 161. (UK edition: SPCK.)

12. N.T. Wright, *The Challenge of Jesus: Rediscovering Who Jesus Was and Is*, Downers Grove: InterVarsity Press, 1999, p. 121. (UK edition: SPCK.)

13. Wright, p. 94.

14. David J. Bosch, *Transforming Mission*, Maryknoll, NY: Orbis, 1991, p. 33.

15. Wright, p. 94.

16. Jurgen Moltmann, *The Future of Creation: Collected Essays,* Minneapolis: Fortress, 1979, p. 118.

17. Walter Brueggemann, *Living Toward a Vision: Biblical Reflections on Shalom*, New York: United Church Press, 1976, p. 18.

18. Thomas Cahill, *The Gift of the Jews*, New York: Doubleday, 1998, pp. 46–47.

19. Cahill, pp. 85–90.

20. M. Douglas Meeks, *God the Economist: The Doctrine of God and the Political Economy*, Minneapolis: Fortress Press, 1989, p. 11.

21. Walter Brueggemann, *Commentary on Isaiah*, Volume 2, 40–66, Westminister Bible Companion, Louisville: Westminister John Knox Press, 1999, p. 18.

The following Bible Verses in this chapter are quoted from *The Message*, by Eugene Peterson, copyright © 1993, 1994, 1995, 1996, NavPress Publishing Group: Isaiah 2:1–4 (page 37), Isaiah 9:2–7 (pages 43–44), Isaiah 40:3–5 (page 53), Isaiah 2:2–5 (page 54) and Isaiah 25: 6–10 (page 55).

3 Living on Purpose: Putting First Things First

For you created my inmost being; you knit me together in my mother's womb.
I praise you because I am fearfully and wonderfully made;
your works are wonderful, I know that full well.
My frame was not hidden from you when I was made in the secret place.
When I was woven together in the depths of the earth, your eyes saw my unformed body.
All the days ordained for me were written in your book before one of them came to be.
How precious to me are your thoughts, O God! How vast is the sum of them!
Were I to count them, they would outnumber the grains of sand, When I awake, I am still with you.
Search me, O God, and know my heart; test me and know my anxious thoughts.
See if there is any offensive way in me, and lead me in the way everlasting.

Psalm 139:13–18, 23–24

The crowd went wild on July 10, 1999 as the American women's soccer team scored the winning goal in a hotly contested game with China. For the first time ever they had won the championship for World Cup Soccer. One cannot read the story of *The Girls of Summer* without being moved by the incredible single-mindedness and discipline of this band of dedicated young women. They set themselves a seemingly unattainable goal and through crushing hard work, pain and determination they won the day. Julie Foudy, one of the members of this remarkable team, wrote, "After all the chaos dies down, when we are old and cranky, don't ever forget the most important element of this tournament. We did it for each other."[1]

They achieved this enormous triumph because they had a strong sense of purpose that called them beyond themselves. For us too, the key to finding a way of life with a difference is to find a purpose for life that calls us beyond ourselves. We strongly believe that none of us will ever find the satisfaction we seek by pursuing the self-involved agendas of Boom City or by simply keeping busy without ever defining our destination. In a Peanuts strip Lucy tells Charlie Brown that she has decided to take up a hobby. He immediately commends her for deciding to accomplish something. To which she responds: "Accomplish something? All I thought we were supposed to do was keep busy."

Finding the focus

We think that deep down inside we all know that life is about more than simply showing up and keeping busy. And I think we also realize we will never find the best God has for us simply by trying to get ahead in our careers and by acquiring a bigger piece of the rock for ourselves and our loved ones. In this chapter we will explain why we will never find the satisfaction we seek by giving our primary allegiance to the upscale aspirations of the Boom City Mall while trying to make it to church once in a while. We are called to get off the freeway and head in another destination . . . toward the City of Shalom.

We will argue that if we really want to find God's best we need to do what Jesus did and give ourselves to a dream that calls us beyond ourselves. If we follow Jesus in making God's purposes our purposes we will discover the possibility of a whole-life faith that is more festive than anything the stress-race can offer. More than that, we will be amazed at how God can use our mustard seed to make a difference in our world.

In this chapter we will also invite you to journey through an "Active Listening Process" to help you discern more clearly a sense of God's call on your life. By the time you complete this chapter hopefully you will have drafted a beginning life mission statement that flows directly out of the shalom purposes of God we discussed in the last chapter. Then in the next chapter we will show you how you can actually use your mission statement to set goals for every part of your life and to reorder your priorities to create a way of life you will truly love.

Putting first things first

In a seminary course called "Faith and Money" the professor asked students to pretend it was their 70th birthday and to write a letter to a loved one from that perspective. The students were asked "to look back over their lives and communicate what they thought was important about the way they lived, particularly in regard to issues of faith and money". This exercise has enabled hundreds of students to decide more intentionally how they want to steward their whole life. The professor reported that students wrote their letters in a way that authentically reflected a serious faith and called them beyond themselves.

One student wrote about how she and her husband intentionally reordered their entire lives to make a difference in the world. They chose to limit their personal lifestyle costs by paying off the small first house they had purchased and not upscaling to a more expensive one. They used the time and money freed up through this and other lifestyle choices to work with the poor and support hunger-related issues. The professor found that students consistently wanted to be faithful to God and generous to others. Most impressively, he stated they all seemed capable of digging down inside themselves and creating imaginative ways to put first things first.[2]

Disciples of Jesus putting first things first

Obviously many of us are going to be a little embarrassed about how we have spent our lives when we blow out those 70 candles if we don't intentionally change the direction of our lives. But the good news is there is still time to put first things first. There

Off Ramp No. 5
Looking back from your 70th birthday

Take the next off ramp and do exactly what the seminary students were asked to do.

1. Write a letter pretending it is your 70th birthday and explain how you have sought over the course of your life to express your faith and use your time and money to put first things first.

2. Now write down how many years you have until your 70th birthday and identify specific ways you could still implement some of the ideas you expressed in your letter of how to put first things first in your life. (If you have already reached your 70th birthday, turn the clock forward as far as you consider realistic!)

3. List two or three initial action steps you would need to take to get started.

4. Finally share your letter with your discussion group or a close Christian friend . . . then share which of those ideas you were considering implementing . . . and ask them to hold you accountable.

is still time to find the best that God has for us and to go for it. So let's look at some of the reasons that many of us have wound up missing the best that God has for us.

Beyond our job as our kingdom vocation

Some of us automatically view our jobs as our kingdom vocation. But as we will show in a later chapter the two are not necessarily the same. Clearly numbers of Christians do find ways to advance God's kingdom purposes through their work in the business world or in their various roles in society. But remember that a number of the disciples in the first century quit their jobs to pursue their Christian vocations.

Beyond the individual pursuit of happiness

We need to recognize that there is a reason many of us have been caught up unwittingly in the huge volume of traffic racing into what really is a land of illusions. There are certainly a spectacular number of consumer goodies in the Boom City Mall but as we have seen that isn't all good news. More and more of us are becoming aware of the hidden price tags we are paying for the "goods life" . . . the hurried sickness, the stress, the constant sense of falling short . . . we are discovering that this race to the top may actually for many of us be a race to the bottom.

One of the primary reasons we got caught up in this mad race is because many of us are persuaded that happiness and fulfilment is something we can attain simply by pursuing it. After all our nation's founding papers talk about the individual "pursuit of happiness". Don't we find the best God has for us by pursuing our own happiness and self-interest? Christian hedonists certainly believe this is the way home. Some of these well-intentioned people have found a way to dress up self-interest and bring it to church. But we are convinced that we can and must move beyond self-interested behaviour and discover, by God's grace, that putting others first is possible.

First, as we have shown, Boom City has seriously misdefined what constitutes happiness. It isn't all about me and satisfying my needs. It isn't all about getting, having and possessing. It isn't about high status or extreme cool. It isn't about scaling that career ladder. It isn't about us enjoying an ever-expanding range of consumer choice. It isn't about me pursuing my own self-interest and simply showing up at church once in a while.

In the City of Shalom we are reminded that God's notion of happiness isn't focused on me and my needs. God's love embraces a world in which people everywhere discover new life in Christ, a world in which our neediest neighbours live without hunger, fear and danger. God intends to welcome all God's children to a grand homecoming celebration in which the blind see, the deaf hear and the lame dance through the streets of the city of God, leading the parade.

Second, as we discussed in the last chapter, as followers of Jesus we aren't called to seek life for ourselves, we are called to lose it. In fact the paradoxical teaching of Jesus is that it is only in losing life that we have any possibility of finding what real life is all about. Listen to Jesus: "If anyone would come after me, he must deny himself and take up his cross daily and follow me. For whoever wants to save his life will lose it, but whoever loses his life for me will save it. What good is it for a man to gain the whole world and yet lose or forfeit his very self?" (Luke 9:23–25).

In other words we will only find the best that God has for us not by pursuing happiness but by losing our lives in service to God and others. Then and only then can we discover the rich, satisfying life that God intends for us. When Christine was preparing to leave her private medical practice in New Zealand in 1980 to follow God's call to set up a medical ministry on the Christian hospital ship the *Anastasis*, she literally walked around her comfortable home up in the hills overlooking Christchurch crying for all she felt that she was giving up. But looking back after 12 years of service on the ship, and remembering how God used her mustard seed to bring healing and hope to the lives of thousands in Africa, Asia and Latin America she realized that far from sacrificing anything she has gained a much more satisfying life than she ever imagined possible.[3] Christine has discovered what so many others are discovering . . . the good life of God is the life given away. Haven't you found particular satisfaction in caring for others?

Where does the good life of God begin? It begins in our willingness to lose our lives in a vision that calls us beyond ourselves . . . seeking first the purposes of God's kingdom in response to the urgent needs in our world. It is important to be clear at this point. God's kingdom is present and coming, both now and not yet. Of course we can't bring the kingdom of God on earth through our own efforts. But the Spirit of the Living God is blowing through the lives of ordinary people all over this planet who are discovering, like Christine, that God can use their mustard seeds to make a difference in the world. Jesus still comes inviting us all to put first things first.

Putting first things first in century one

Jesus couldn't have been clearer about what was entailed in becoming one of his followers, "So do not worry, saying, 'What shall we eat?' or 'What shall we drink?' or 'What shall we wear?' For the pagans run after all these things, and your heavenly Father knows that you need them. But seek first his kingdom and his righteousness, and all these things will be given to you as well" (Matthew 6:31–33). In other words the primary focus for disciples of Christ is not in providing for our physical needs, as legitimate as those are, but rather in seeking first the kingdom purposes of God.

In fact it appears from the gospels and the book of Acts that there wasn't any real differentiation between "pastors", "missionaries" and everyone else. Those first followers believed all of them were called to a more radical whole-life faith in which reaching out to others was central. The overarching mission statement for all followers of Jesus was what missiologist David Bosch calls "the language of love that was on their lips and in their lives."[4]

Paul reminds us ". . . we are God's workmanship, created in Christ Jesus to do good works, which God prepared in advance for us to do" (Ephesians 2:10). In other words the reason we are on this planet is not to simply try to increase the profits of a corporation, buy a nice home, get our kids off to their activities and try to make it to church once in a while. The Creator God has prepared us to do the good works of God's new shalom order. OK: if we are prepared to do God's good works where do we begin?

Discovering how to make God's purposes our purposes

In the introduction we mentioned that most Christians have no idea how to connect whatever Sunday morning and the sermon is about to our lives seven days a week. So most of us have no idea how to put God's purposes first, even if we wanted to. But some have managed to find a connection between their Sunday faith and their lives seven days a week, and we want to share a few examples. These are people who, like those first disciples, have found the satisfaction of *living on purpose.*

The Sittsers

Jerry Sittser suffered an incredible tragedy ten years ago. He lost his wife, one of his children and his mother in a violent automobile crash. Left as a single parent with three kids to bring up on his own he struggled to make sense of the enormity of his tragedy. He wanted to find a way out of that painful event to honour those who had died. He decided to sit down with his three remaining kids and hammer out a family mission statement to raise them on purpose.

As a theologian teaching at Whitworth College in Spokane, Washington, Jerry knew how to use scripture to draft a mission statement and he fully involved his kids in the exercise. They also developed a weekly meeting to reflect on their family mission statement. Before, like most Christian families, their only sense of direction was to try to make it from Monday to Sunday. Now they have found a way to make God's purposes their purposes . . . for their entire family.

I recently phoned Jerry and asked, "What difference has the family mission statement made for your family over the past ten years?" He responded that this past summer he was invited to lecture at Daystar in Kenya. He decided to take his three kids with him . . . Catherine (18), David (13) and John (11). In keeping with their mission statement his children spent two days a week volunteering at a Mother Theresa Orphanage for disabled and abandoned kids. One morning Jerry finished his lectures early and decided to look in on his kids. John was sitting quietly in a corner rocking a small malnourished baby in his arms. Catherine was singing while she fed five badly disabled kids who had been abandoned by their parents. Jerry told me he was very proud of his kids. And on their return home to Spokane, they decided to do some service projects together as a family every month to keep the flame shining. Jerry confided that if he hadn't written a mission statement with his kids a decade before they would never have embarked on a course as a family that called them beyond themselves.

Max De Pree

We find that a growing number of Christian businessmen who routinely use mission statements in their business are beginning to live out their Christian faith in their workplace more intentionally. When Max De Pree was chairman of the Herman Miller Corporation he sought to bring his biblical faith and sense of Christian calling to bear on a number of different aspects of his business. For example, he placed a cap on executive salaries in his firm. Then he laboured aggressively to improve compensation for workers on the bottom rung of the corporate ladder.

Ivan

Ivan is a Christian businessman in Melbourne, Australia, who decided several years ago to put God's purposes first in his life. He told us that before he wrote his mission statement his life was paralysed by busyness, fear and an overwhelming sense of his own brokenness. Then he drafted his mission statement, which reads: "I commit my life to partnering with God in projecting God's love to the unloved." He started using his leisure time to work with disabled kids, even passing up promotions to protect his time for his ministry with these kids he loved. Today he and his wife have started a small business to enable them to free up even more time for the kids. Ivan told us: "Once I had resolved to live my life with God's purposes at the centre everything was transformed. I never have been more at peace with myself or more fulfilled." The good life of God is indeed the life given away.

Christine and Tom

As a result of Christine's work amongst the poor in Africa, Asia and South America and Tom's mission work in Haiti we have both developed a compelling desire to see something of God's kingdom come among our poorest neighbours. Our joint mission statement comes from Proverbs 31:8–9: "Speak up for those who cannot speak for themselves, for the rights of all who are destitute. Speak up and judge fairly; defend the rights of the poor and needy." Our mission statement reads "To become a voice for those who have no voice and bring glimpses of God's shalom kingdom into people's lives."

We work together as consultants for churches and mission organizations helping Christians, churches and Christian organizations to create imaginative ways to put God's purposes first in responses to the new challenges of our rapidly changing future. The content of what we share comes directly out of our mission statement . . . being advocates for the poor, the forgotten and those at the margins. But as you will see, our statement impacts all areas of our lives as well.

Finding God's mission statement for your life

As you know nature abhors a vacuum. If we aren't as intentional in setting a biblical focus for our lives as the examples we have just shared . . . you can be sure that other forces will step in and set the direction of our lives for us. And the forces most likely to take over are the acquisitive impulses of Boom City Mall rather than the compassionate motivations of the City of Shalom.

Where to start? If we are deadly serious about finding God's best for our lives it doesn't begin with the question "what do I want and what turns me on?" but "what does God want and how does God want to use my mustard seed to make a difference in the world?" It is our firm conviction that God doesn't just call ministers and missionaries to make a difference for God's kingdom. Every disciple of Jesus is called to a whole-life faith in which mission is at the centre of our lives and families instead of at the margins. The people we know who enjoy life the most are those who are discovering, like the Sittser family, how God wants to use their mustard seed to make a difference in the world.

One of the most frequent questions we hear Christian college students ask is: "How in the world can I find God's will for my life?" But many of the standard approaches to discernment from waiting for doors to open to putting out "fleeces" have had very mixed results for Christians of all ages. We are proposing a very different approach to discerning God's will that enables you to directly connect your life to a sense of God's biblical mission purposes. We come across so many talented committed people, of all generations, who have no idea of God's call on their lives. We believe that the problem is that either God isn't speaking or we are not listening so well. Of course God is speaking to us all the time in many different ways. So obviously we need to become much better listeners.

Three hundred years ago Quakers created a process called "listening for clearness". It provides a process for listening more carefully to God's leading in our lives and churches. Well-known Quaker author Parker Palmer, in his book *Let Your Life Speak: Listening for the Voice of Vocation,* encourages us "to listen to what our lives are saying *and* take notes on it, lest we forget our own truth or deny that we ever heard it".[5] We need to learn to hear what God is saying to us through our own lives, the lives of others and particularly through scripture.

We want to invite you to take the next off ramp and join us in this Active Listening Process[6] we have created to assist you to gain a clearer sense of God's call on your life. This exercise has the single purpose of *assisting you to write a beginning mission statement to enable you to put first things first.*

Off Ramp No. 6
Listening for God's best

Step one – Retreat from the distractions of Boom City

We realize that many readers are stressed out trying to keep up with the traffic racing towards the seductive skyline of Boom City. When there is so much noise and distraction, like cell phones, walkmans, and TVs blaring in the background, it is hard to hear anything from God. As Morton T. Kelsey comments in *The Other Side of Silence: A Guide to Christian Meditation* "In contemporary society our Adversary majors in three things: noise, hurry and crowds. If he can keep us engaged in 'muchness' and 'manyness' he will rest satisfied. Psychiatrist C. G. Jung once remarked, 'Hurry is not *of* the Devil; it *is* the Devil'."[7]

In order to hear from God we need to take serious time to listen. If we are ready to join Jesus Christ in putting first things first then we must begin where Jesus did . . . in prayer. The most self-evident characteristic of Jesus' prayer life was that he went on prayer retreats . . . extended times alone with God. This seems to be where Jesus not only spent intimate moments with the God who called him but where God revealed to Jesus the call on his life. If the Son of God needed to take serious times off for prayer retreats to hear God's call then we certainly need to.

The journey towards whole-life faith begins for all of us in the place of prayer. It can be very helpful to retreat and get away from all the distractions. There are many Protestant and Catholic retreat facilities available in most of our communities. Or you could always find an inexpensive cabin, bed and breakfast or motel to retreat to. Book a weekend. If you have kids, find a willing baby sitter and escape the stress-race in order to free up time to listen to God's call on your life. At least try to find a few hours on a weekend or in the evening to do a mini-retreat. We go on quarterly retreats. One of our favourite spots is the island of Iona off the West Coast of Scotland. It was from here that the Celtic monks went out two by two, spreading the gospel throughout Britain and then into Europe. It has become something of a spiritual home for us, and its rich Christian history provides a challenging reminder for us as we seek to refocus our own lives. We find we need two full days to really listen carefully to God. Whether you are able to get away for a weekend or for a mini-retreat during the week, the sole purpose is to listen for God's call on your entire life.

Find your place of retreat freed from distractions of daily life so you can listen carefully to God. Take your Bible and journal. Begin the process by writing the following question at the top of your journal page: "How does God want to use my life to work for God's purposes?" After you settle in, pray that God will help you listen to the many ways God calls us.

Step two – Listening for the call of God in stillness

For many of us the most difficult step in the Active Listening Process is one that we don't even think of as "active" – learning to clear our minds of the concerns of the world we live in so that we are able to listen to what God is saying to us. Take some time up front and consciously release all those pressures and seductions to God so you can listen without distraction for God's call on your life. Once you have fully cleared the decks, relax and sit in silence, simply enjoying the presence of God. Reflect on all you have to be grateful for and give thanks for God's many graces in your life. Meditating on scripture and reminding ourselves of God's constant care for us not only redirects our thoughts to God but also fills us with gratitude and instills an expectation that God will come and speak to us now in our present situation too.

Step three – Listening for God's voice in our past

Christine loves the story of Samuel in the first few chapters of 1 Samuel. He was dedicated to God by his mother Hannah before he was born. And he was called by God as a child even before he fully understood what the voice of God sounded like (1 Samuel 3:2–9). God calls to many of us from a very early age; sometimes even before we are aware of our need to follow Christ. From the time Christine was a young child she loved to travel and was intrigued by the life stories of missionaries. As a teenager she read *Ten Fingers for God*, the story of Paul and Margaret Brand: two Christian doctors who pioneered the work of tendon transplants amongst lepers in India.[8] This is one of her earliest memories of the call of God into medical missions . . . years before she committed her life to Christ.

Journey backwards in your own story and try to identify some of your earliest memories of God's call on your life. Were you dedicated to God as a child? If so, ask your parents about their impression of God's call on your life at that time. Did you sense a particular call to work with the urban poor, become a missionary, an artist or a musician? Then write down in your journal everything you remember of that earliest sense of God's call on your life. Next, write down the specific ways that God has used your life as a child, young person or young adult to touch someone else or to make a little difference in your world. One young woman reflects that as a youth she came alive when she sat with the homeless on the streets and listened to their stories. But it had never occurred to her that this might be a part of God's call on her life.

Step four – Listening for God's call through the scripture

The most important way God speaks to us and calls us is through scripture. Through studying scripture we can learn what God is doing and join it. In the last chapter we looked at the compelling imagery of the biblical vision of God's loving shalom purposes for a people and a world. Go back and review the chapter meditating particularly on the scripture about God's mission purposes. Remember how Jesus and his friends related their lives to God's purposes.

Look over the pictures you drew in the last chapter of how the coming of God's shalom into your life or the lives of those you care about might make a difference. Picture a world in which justice finally comes for the poor, peace comes to the nations and wholeness to those who are broken. Picture yourself in the middle of these images. Quite apart from this book and the scripture we used, how has God been speaking to you in recent days through the Bible in your private time or at church? Write down all that you hear God saying to you through scripture . . . particularly as it relates to connecting your life to God's mission purposes.

Step five – Listening to God's call through prayer

In step three we asked you how you sensed God had called you in your childhood. Now we want to ask: "How do you sense God is calling you through prayer today?" The prophet Isaiah had a life-changing encounter with the Living God in the temple. After the initial encounter Isaiah heard the Lord saying "Whom shall I send? And who will go for us?" and Isaiah responded "Here am I. Send me!" (Isaiah 6:8). After Mark and Claire Dowds, a young couple from Ireland, returned from speaking at a conference in Vancouver BC on "Church and the Youth Culture" Claire sensed in prayer that God had new plans for their lives. She told Mark that she believed God was calling them to return to Vancouver to minister. Mark was dubious but the more he prayed the more he sensed a call from God as well. The very next day he got a call from BC inviting him and Claire to come and work with young leaders there. That call sealed it, and they headed to Vancouver.

Write down how you believe God has been calling you through prayer.

Step six – Listening to God through the needs of others

One of the most important but least mentioned ways God calls us is through the needs, pain and suffering of others. Working in the refugee camps in Thailand in the early 1980s was a pivotal experience in Christine's life. She still remembers the horror of people suffering starvation, torture or rape in their flight from the genocide in Cambodia and the trauma of emaciated children dying in her arms. This tragic experience became central in God's call on her life to be a voice for those who have no voice. Tom's experience of working with the poor in Haiti for World Concern had the same impact on his life and sense of calling.

What human needs tear at your heart? They may very well be God's call on your life. Is it kids in your community caught in the grip of drugs and alcohol addiction? Is it the plight of lonely seniors and shut-ins? Is it AIDS orphans in Uganda? Mother Teresa said it best, "Jesus is often thinly disguised in the poor and the suffering in our midst." Write down those areas of human need that most tug at your heart . . . they may be God's call on your life.

Step seven – Listen to your gifts and talents

Do you want to find God's call on your life? Then pay attention to how God has gifted you. God hasn't gifted us to increase corporate profits or to pursue lavish lifestyles. God has gifted us for the kingdom. As Elizabeth O'Connor reminds us in her book *Eighth Day of Creation: Gifts and Creativity*: "Our gifts are on loan. We are responsible for spending them in the world and we will be held accountable."[9] She also tells us "When I become aware of my own gifts and give my attention to communicating what is in me – my own truth, as it were – I have the experience of growing toward wholeness. I am working out God's 'chosen purpose' and I am no longer dependent on what others think and how they respond."[10] So write down your areas of giftedness and don't be modest. The giftings of God are rich and varied. Are you good at administration, or at organizing people? Do you enjoy working with computers or do you thrive at developing relationships? Perhaps you are a gifted teacher or public speaker. Whatever your gifts are, write them down. Then reflect on opportunities that you have had to develop these gifts through education, employment or ministry.

Second, God has blessed all of us with creative gifts that are meant to enrich our understanding of God's kingdom. For example, Christine loves gardening and Tom loves to cook international food. Perhaps you are gifted in writing songs or painting pictures. Barbara is a talented Australian artist, but she had never considered her painting as a gift to be used to give expression to God's kingdom. Then a few years ago she had an opportunity to visit sites in the Australian outback where aboriginals had been massacred. She felt the land cry out with the ghosts of those who had perished. Her creative gift came alive in evocative and haunting paintings that have not only raised awareness of the aboriginal plight but have also laid foundations for reconciliation with white Australians. Write down your creative gifts.

We are all gifted spiritually too. Paul reminds us that "just as each of us has one body with many members, and these members do not all have the same function, so in Christ we who are many form one body, and each member belongs to all the others. We have different gifts, according to the grace given us" (Romans 12:4–6) and then again "It was he [Christ] who gave some to be apostles, some to be prophets, some to be evangelists, and some to be pastors and teachers, to prepare God's people for works of service, so that the body of Christ may be built up" (Ephesians 4:11–12). Write down your spiritual gifts that you are aware of and the ways these have been developed through involvement in your church, in your community and in ministry to others.

There are many resources available to help identify your gifts. One that we have found particularly helpful is *LifeKeys,* by Jane Kise, David Stark and Sandra Krebs Hirsh.[11] It provides a comprehensive guide to discovering your talents, spiritual gifts and passions.

Step eight – Listening to God's call on our lives through the broken places

Corporate head hunters are always looking for the brightest and best. The amazing thing about the kingdom is that God can often use our failures and broken places to advance more effectively the kingdom than our gifts. God really does delight in taking the foolish things of the world to confound the wise. Charles Colson started Prison Fellowship not because of his gifts but because he was a felon imprisoned for his part in the Watergate cover-up. Joni Erickson Tada suffered a terrible swimming accident as a teenager that left her paralysed from the neck down. From the world's perspective her life was now useless but God has used her to develop an incredible ministry to disabled people around the world because of her own brokenness.

Candidly write down your areas of brokenness, addiction or disability. Were you orphaned or abused as a child? Have you suffered the pain of divorce or the death of a loved one? Have you lost your job and become homeless? Do you struggle with drug addiction or alcoholism? God can transform whatever is broken in your life into tools for the kingdom.

Step nine – Listening to God's call on your life through your dreams

In his helpful book *What Color is your Parachute?* Richard Nelson Bolles reminds us "Most of us have our visions and dream our dreams. It's only when we come to our job, and what we want to do with the rest of our lives, that we think our visions and dreams must be shelved."[12] Most of us do have dreams about our future that may seem far-fetched or unrealistic so we ignore them. Yet often they are God's promptings, meant to nudge us in a direction that is very different from what our life has taken to this point. Write down your unfulfilled possibilities and dreams and describe ways in which these might be a reflection of God's call on your life.

Step ten – Listening to God's call on your life through your imagination

Now it's creativity time. We do Creativity Workshops with people in churches, college students and educators and we are convinced one of the least used gifts in the church today is our creativity. Invite the Spirit of the living God to blow through your imagination and pull together everything you have written down to this point in this Active Listening Process.

Start with a new sheet of paper. At the top of the page write down the sense of biblical purposes you listed in step No. 4. It is essential that your sense of vocation is as clearly connected as Jesus' was to the shalom purposes of God. Begin to imagine different ways those purposes could be expressed in and through your life. Now prayerfully read all the other things you have written down in this Active Listening Process regarding how God is speaking to you through prayer, the needs of others, your gifts and brokenness. Brainstorm at least three different ways these might converge into a single vocation. Write down these possibilities and pray over them for wisdom.

Step eleven – Listening to God through picturing new possibilities

Now for the challenging part. Prayerfully select from these three different possibilities the one that seems truest to your sense of God's call on your life. Using coloured pens if you have them, draw a picture that brings your sense of God's call vitally to life. Try to make your picture as vivid and detailed as possible until you can see, touch and taste your emerging sense of vocation. Share your three possibilities from the last step and your picture from this exercise with people in your study group or with a Christian friend. Ask them to pray with you for clarity and confirmation as you begin to work on a beginning mission statement.

Drafting a biblical mission statement

Now you have the wonderful opportunity to take the hard work you did in the Active Listening Process in off ramp exercise 6, particularly your work in the final two steps, and work on a biblical mission statement that reflects your best sense of God's call on your life. We have worked with a number of groups of Christians, many of whom have, in a two-hour listening process, made a beginning. They have actually put pen to paper and drafted beginning mission statements that have helped them find that sense of purpose for their lives they had been seeking. Let us offer some guidelines.

A few guidelines for drafting a mission statement

1. First write down at the top of your page those scripture passages that most directly connect your life to the shalom purposes of God. Ask God's guidance as you begin this process.
2. Working from your last two steps in the Active Listening Process, particularly your picture, try in a sentence or two to draft a beginning mission statement that summarizes your best sense of God's call. Remember that biblically based mission statements differ from the usual mission statements in that they focus outwardly on God's purposes to make a difference in our world instead of inwardly on satisfying our own needs. Try to incorporate scripture so that your statement clearly reveals something of God's loving purposes for the larger world.
3. Remember, mission statements are meant to be inspirational and fill us with enthusiasm. "So often we find ourselves asking, *What is wrong?* The more important question is *How does God want to make this right and what can I do to be part of God's solution to this problem?* Finding the positive spin on a negative situation is the redemptive edge of purpose in life," explains Jan Johnson.[13]
4. One of the mistakes many of us make when we put together

our mission statements is that we want to include too much. Too often we try to incorporate our goals, strategies and our "to do lists" as well as our overall sense of purpose. On one occasion a young man named Brent told Christine "This mission statement business never worked for me. I wrote one two years ago and never followed it." She asked to see his statement and much to her surprise he produced a four-page document! No wonder he had never looked at it.

5. Just like any road map, a mission statement needs to be clear, concise and easy to follow. Ideally, according to Laurie Beth Jones, there are three elements to a good mission statement: it "should be no more than a sentence long, should be easily understood by a twelve year old, and should be able to be recited by memory at gun point."[14]

6. While it should be short and concise it also needs to be broad enough to influence every single area of our lives. Jan Johnson explains "I prefer general mission statements that don't name specific tasks. Broad wording that assumes the purposes will permeate every role in life . . . Your purposes are more than what you *do*; they encompass who God has called you to *be*."[15] We all need a 24/7 mission statement not just for our spiritual life or ministry. We need a statement that helps us re-focus our lives in terms of our relationships with friends, family and the folks we go to church with. We even need a statement that can help us with the important life choices regarding how we steward our time and money and the choices we make as consumers.

7. As we move toward our calling we will begin to experience that more fulfilling way of life God intends for us. For some this calling will be expressed in our workplaces, for others in our homes and neighbourhoods. Some may be called to relocate. Wherever God calls us to advance the purposes of the kingdom our mission statement should wake us up every morning and send us charging into the day with a fresh sense of excitement.

Mission statements make a difference

Rebuilding lives with Maureen

Maureen's mission statement included the biblical call to "reclaim the land and rebuild the walls" as mentioned in Isaiah 58:12. She has walked through the deaths of both her parents and a couple of close friends in the last few years and these painful experiences helped shape her sense of mission call. She is now studying to be a counsellor because she wants to use the pain of her own bereavements to encourage and support others who are going through the death or prolonged illness of those they love.

Recycling lives with Fred

Fred is a Christian businessman whose mission statement led him not only to start a recycling business to help care for creation but also to reach out to those who had been excluded from the workplace by their disabilities. Fred found disabled people made great employees and were highly motivated. Through his small business he was able to work for two of the goals of God's kingdom . . . restoration of both excluded lives and God's creation.

Partying the kingdom with Paul

Paul, an accountant, is a real party person. He is enthusiastic to see expressions of the celebration of God's kingdom in his community, particularly in the lives of the poor, whom he feels are often unfairly treated by others. His biblical mission statement reads "to be God's Jubilee in the community". Paul is involved in setting up a kingdom bank within the community so that poor people can borrow money without paying exorbitant rates of interest. He is also planning a street fair and a kingdom banquet as expressions of God's kingdom celebration.

Finding our way home to living on purpose

We are convinced that we can all find God's best if we are willing to listen. We can find a way of life that makes a difference . . . a way of life that is much more festive and satisfying than anything offered at Boom City.

How are you doing? Were you able to draft a beginning mission statement? How do you feel about this possible new beginning in your life? In the next two chapters we will help you start to put wheels under your mission statement and get rolling in a new direction. We will show you in Chapter 4 specific ways to set goals for your entire life that reflect your mission statement. In Chapter 5 we will also outline creative ways you can reinvent your timestyle and lifestyle to create a fuller, more satisfying, way of life that will make a little difference in the world.

Notes

1. Jere Longman, *The Girls of Summer*, New York: Harper & Row, 2000, p. 307.
2. James Hudnut-Beumler, *Generous Saints*, West Bethesda, MD: The Alban Institute, 1999, p. 115.
3. Christine's adventures on board the *Anastasis* are recounted in *Confessions of a Seasick Doctor*, Christine Aroney-Sine, Crowborough, UK: Monarch Books, 1995.
4. David J. Bosch, *Transforming Mission*, Maryknoll, NY: Orbis, 1991, p. 191.
5. Parker J. Palmer, *Let Your Life Speak: Listening for the Voice of Vocation*, San Francisco: Jossey-Bass, 2000, p. 6.
6. Adapted from Tom Sine, *Live It Up! How to Create a Life You Can Love*, Scottsdale: Herald Press, 1993.
7. Morton T. Kelsey, *The Other Side of Silence: A Guide to Christian Meditation*, London: SPCK: 1977.
8. Dorothy Clarke Wilson, *Ten Fingers for God: The Life and Work of Dr Paul Brand*, Seattle Wa, Paul Brand Publishing, 1989.

9. Elizabeth O'Connor, *Eighth Day of Creation: Gifts and Creativity*, Waco: Word, 1977, p. 23.

10. O'Connor, p. 15.

11. Jane A. G. Kise, David Stark, Sandra Krebs Hirsh, *LifeKeys: Discovering Who You Are, Why You're Here, What You Do Best*, Minneapolis: Bethany House Publishers, 1996.

12. Richard N. Bolles, *What Color is Your Parachute?*, Berkeley: Ten Speed Press, 1977, p. 92.

13. Jan Johnson, *Living a Purpose Full Life*, Colorado Springs, CO: Waterbrook Press, 1999, p. 85.

14. Laurie Beth Jones, *The Path: Creating Your Mission Statement for Work and for Life*, New York: Hyperion, 1996.

15. Johnson, p. 85.

4 Living on Purpose: Setting Goals for a Whole-life Faith

I am giving you worship with my whole life,
I am giving you assent with my whole power,
I am giving you praise with my whole tongue
I am giving you reverence with my whole understanding
I am giving you love with my whole heart.[1]

It was Katie's first visit to an American toy store. She and her dad Mike were visiting from England and she had never seen anything like the Disney World Toy Store before. Katie is a very sophisticated little lady for a seven year old but she was still intrigued by the huge selection of toys. She quietly picked them up, examined them and then very carefully put them back down. As they completed their tour of the huge store Mike looked back over his shoulder and spied an attendant systematically placing every doll, toy or game Katie had examined during her 30-minute tour in a cart . . . apparently fully expecting to make a huge sale.

When they arrived at the checkout counter Katie noticed the attendant with her cart stuffed full like Santa's sleigh, for the first time. She turned and smiled courteously. "Thank you very much," she said, "but I really think we need to look around at other shops a bit more." Mike watched as the clerk visibly deflated. Mike told us that in spite of her age Katie is very savvy about the consumer culture and sees right through its efforts to manipulate her into buying things she neither wants nor needs. She is content simply to look and explore what is happening in the world around her without expecting her dad to buy her something every time they go out.

Finding the focus

In this chapter we will try to become as wise as little Katie and more fully take charge of our lives and choices. We will do this by exploring the possibilities of a whole-life faith in which our choices come much more directly out of a biblical faith instead of simply being dull reflections of the dominant culture. We will argue that the choice to follow Jesus Christ involves a much more substantial change in every part of our lives than we talk about in many of our churches. We find the postmodern young are looking for a much more vital whole-life faith that flows into every part of their lives.

As part of this journey towards a more serious whole-life faith we will invite you to identify the unstated goals that seem to direct your life right now. And then we will invite you to use your beginning mission statement to draft goals for every part of your life . . . goals that look more like the hope City of Shalom than the illusory promises of Boom City. This is your opportunity to give flesh and blood to your mission statement. It is your opportunity to take charge of your life and no longer be captive to other people's pressures and expectations. This is your opportunity to find the best that God has for you . . . a more vital whole-life faith. And as you begin to both draft and implement new goals I think you will discover a way of life that is not only less stressed but also much fuller, more festive and satisfying than you ever dreamed possible.

An invitation to escape to reality

Trapped in the land of illusions

The film *The Matrix* begins in a world that looks very much like our world. But Neo, the hero, is startled to discover that it isn't the real world at all. It is an illusory world created by machines and beamed into the minds of human beings to keep them happy while they live out their lives in nutrient vats. Neo discovers that he and his compatriots lying cosily in their wombs are actually being used as the food supply for a race of sentient machines. Outside this world of illusion however, he discovers, there is another world, the real world, a place in which a small group of people live and fight in hope of freedom and release for all of humanity.

It is one thing for Neo to catch a glimpse of the real world, but another for him to escape his captivity. And when he makes the very costly choice to break out of this world of illusions into the real world he discovers that outside his womblike vat is a very challenging place to live. We believe that like Neo we are all trapped in an illusory world. But most of us aren't as aware as Neo or as discerning as little Katie of the ways we are being manipulated. And those of us who are more aware of our captivity don't have much of an idea how to escape from the upside-down world of the land of illusions to the right-side-up world of the land of the Shalom of God. Let us share a story about one suburban mother who was largely oblivious to her family's captivity.

Several years ago Tom was speaking to a group of parents whose kids go to the Christian high school in a very upscale community in Pennsylvania. He tried to make them aware of the influence of the illusory values of their very affluent community on themselves and their kids. Tom said, "I believe the hardest place to raise kids with Christian values is the affluent suburbs of America because in these communities the young are under relentless pressure to wear the same expensive designer brands, hit the resort ski slopes on the same weekend and derive their sense of identity from deeply reinforced notions of style, image and status."

Predictably some of the parents were upset by his remarks. One of the mums, Judy, really got angry and scolded Tom for "his unwarranted attack on her community". Then she changed the subject and said: "For over six weeks my daughter who is a junior at New Life School hasn't talked to her dad or myself." "Why not?" Tom asked. Judy responded, "She won't talk to us because she has to be seen being driven to school in a car that is three years old . . . Can you explain her behaviour?" Tom exclaimed, "That was the point I was trying to make. You didn't just buy a nice home in this affluent suburban neighbourhood. You bought all the upscale and high-status values that go with your community. Don't you see if you had bought a home in Pittsburgh or in the small farming community down the road from here, your daughter would be glad to have a ride to school in any kind of vehicle?" Have you seen this kind of neighbourhood influence?

Like most parents Judy and her husband wanted what's best for their daughter. Like many sincere Christian parents they tend to define what's best largely in economic terms. They chose this community because they wanted to give their daughter the "best". Like Judy, many of us unwittingly allow the values of the dominant culture that we call Boom City, instead of the values of our faith, to define what is best for ourselves and for our kids.

Finding our way home to the right-side-up values of the kingdom

Where do we find our exit out of this illusory world of Boom City to the real world of vital whole-life faith? Where do we begin our trek out of this upside-down world to the right-side-up world of the City of Shalom? There is no switch to flick to help us come down off the ceiling and get our feet back on the ground again. Only as we begin to wake up to the many different ways the dominant culture has shaped our aspirations and values, is there any hope of coming home to a biblical faith that transforms every part of our lives.

Just as Neo's journey into reality began with a new birth, so must ours. We all begin at the foot of the Cross of Christ. This is not just the place where we lay down our moral failings and spiritual shortcomings. It is the place where we must also lay down our illusory notion of what's best and all the cultural programming we have been subjected to. One of the first places to start is to recognize that many churches are operating from a deeply flawed concept of what it means to be a disciple of Jesus Christ.

Off Ramp No. 7

Checking out your unstated goals

It is time to stop and take a quick audit of the unstated values that direct our lives and shape our goals. Let's start by looking at the notion of what is "best" in your community.

1. Take a tour of your neighbourhood, your local shopping centre and your church parking lot on Sunday morning and make a list of what seem to be the values behind the cars, houses and stores. What appears to be the implicit notion of what is "best?" If you can, video what you are seeing along with your running analysis to share with others.

2. Attempt to list what appear to be some of the unstated goals in people's lives as they are reflected in the neighbourhood they live in, the cars they drive and the places they shop. Describe any difference you see in the unstated goals of your Christian and non-Christian neighbours.

3. Now, take a good hard look at your own life. What are your unstated goals and how are these unstated goals influencing your life priorities?

4. Share what you have learned through this audit with your group or a friend. Identify which implicit goals in your life you might want to change to more authentically reflect the values of your faith instead of those of the dominant culture.

Rediscovering the possibility of whole-life discipleship

Doing discipleship on a two-legged stool

Today almost all the models of discipleship we teach in our churches and take around the world through our mission programmes fall seriously short, we believe, of the biblical model. Many churches have settled for a compartmentalized piety in which both mainline and evangelical churches quietly sanction the values of modern culture instead of challenging them. We

believe that this is one of the primary reasons for our compartmentalized faith and our dualistic discipleship.

The standard approach to discipleship is in trouble because
it seeks to operate on a very unstable two-legged milk stool.
Anyone who has ever milked cows by hand knows you can use
a three-legged stool or even a one-legged stool but a two-legged
stool is inherently unstable. The legs on the two-legged standard model of discipleship are:

1. Spiritual transformation . . . getting our hearts right with God;
2. Moral transformation . . . getting our moral act together.

Both are absolutely essential to vital biblical faith. But we are
missing a very important third leg.

We believe scripture teaches that God wants to transform us
not only spiritually and morally but culturally too. To be biblical disciples we need to put a third leg on our stool. We can no
longer do our discipleship over the top of the individualism,
materialism, consumerism and status-driven values of Boom
City and wind up with anything that looks like authentic biblical faith. The call to follow Jesus has always been a call to
radical whole-life discipleship.

Following Jesus into a counter-cultural faith

Jesus' call to whole-life discipleship was laser clear. He didn't
invite his disciples to a private pietism they could work in
around the edges of lives largely shaped by the dominant
culture. "He called the crowd to him along with his disciples
and said: 'If anyone would come after me, he must deny himself
and take up his cross and follow me. For whoever wants to save
his life will lose it, but whoever loses his life for me and for the
gospel will save it. What good is it for a man to gain the whole
world, yet forfeit his soul?'" (Mark 8:34–36). The call to follow
Christ was an invitation to a whole-life faith that was pro-
foundly counter-cultural both then and now. Those first disciples never settled for the kind of narrow, disengaged faith that

has become normative today. They understood that following Jesus was a whole-life proposition. And those earliest disciples had absolutely no doubt that following this Jesus required them to put a third leg on their discipleship stool and be transformed not only spiritually and morally, but *culturally* too.

Jesus' teachings and the character of the common life he shared with that first community of disciples are as radically counter-cultural today as they were in the first century. Jesus taught us that losing is winning, the last shall be first and the way to deal with violence is to turn the other cheek. He told us we were to love our enemies, forgive our friends and learn from little children about the coming of God's new order. He renounced the pursuit of wealth and power, washed feet, cared for the broken and hung out with the most disreputable members of his society.

"In short," Rodney Clapp insists, the early church understood itself as "a new unique culture".[2] It was radically different from the dominant culture in which it was planted. Believers became part of a new community, and Christianity created communities that were very different from the society around them. These new right-side-up communities modelled a new culture that united Jew and Gentile, male and female, slave and free into a new kind of relationship which demonstrated "the practice of love and service to all".[3] "They crossed cultural and ethnic boundaries. They evoked radical changes in the practice of land ownership and personal wealth, established common treasuries, and mandated the sharing of all worldly resources."[4]

Following Jesus into the creation of a new way

The historical evidence suggests that the earliest followers of Jesus saw themselves as belonging to a new culture, "a third race" neither Jew nor Gentile but a new and holy nation or people.[5] They took very seriously Paul's admonition "Do not conform any longer to the pattern of this world, but be transformed by the renewing of your mind. Then you will be able to test and approve what God's will is – his good, pleasing and perfect will" (Romans 12:2). For them the call to no longer "be

conformed to the patterns of this world" wasn't just a call to be
morally different from the pagan society around them but actually to be culturally distinct as well.

Wayne Meeks, exploring the earliest origins of our Christian
faith, reinforces this view that becoming a follower of Christ
required a much more radical commitment that resulted in a
more profound cultural transformation than today. He
declares, "Becoming a Christian meant something like the
experience of an immigrant who leaves his or her native land
and then assimilates to the culture of a new, adopted homeland."[6] A very radical change indeed!

Today, we need to create imaginative ways to reach people
with the good news in whatever culture we find them, whether
it is the pierced and tatooed culture of the streets or the affluent
culture of suburban estates. Instead of simply offering them a
little private piety that is largely disconnected from the rest of
their lives we are advocates offering a whole-life faith that
invites them to become part of a new family and a new culture.
We propose helping them to put a third leg on their discipleship
stool by inviting God to transform not only their spiritual and
moral values but their cultural values too. We believe that only
as the contemporary church becomes a counter-cultural presence in society again will we, like those who have gone before us,
begin to have a compelling witness for God's radical kingdom.

Recalling our legacy of a whole-life faith

Many of our predecessors in the faith seemed to understand
more clearly than we do today that they were called to a whole-
life faith meant to transform every part of life. At the centre of
this whole-life faith was a decisive movement from a self-
interested life to one that is extended in compassion to our
neighbours near and far. And these models were also a compelling counterpoint to the societies in which they found themselves. In fact many of them are still powerfully impacting the
lives of people today because of their ringing authenticity.

Saint Patrick

In the fifth century, a young Englishman by the name of Patrick became a devoted evangelist to the Irish because he had a dream in which a man came to him from Ireland bearing a letter entitled "The Voice of the Irish". As he read the letter he heard the voices of many Irish people beckoning him to come and walk among them.[7] It is amazing that he actually heeded that call because not long before Patrick had been kidnapped from his home in England to work as a slave in Ireland. But in spite of his captivity Patrick accepted God's call. And as a result of the enthusiastic and vigorous evangelistic work of Patrick and the Celtic Christians who followed him, thousands were converted to Christ, hundreds of churches were planted and Ireland was successfully evangelized in three decades. Not only were the lives of individuals transformed, but so was the culture they were a part of.

These Irish monks followed Christ's call and planted churches and monastic communities throughout Scotland, England and Europe. For the Celtic monks, there was no greater privilege than to "wander for the Lord" on *peregrinatio*, turning their backs on their homes and their possessions in order to carry the good news of Christ throughout the world. Much to our amazement, when we were in Switzerland a few years ago we came across a small chapel on the shores of Lake Thun which had been established by two Irish missionaries in the seventh century.

For these Celtic Christians, faith was the cohesive force that held together all of their lives. Even for ordinary believers who never left their homes, faith pervaded every area of life. They had prayers for everything from kindling a fire to milking the cows, prayers that made their entire lives a liturgy before God.[8]

Francis of Assisi

St Francis of Assisi was another who understood that following Jesus required a total transformation of every part of his life. Francis began life as an affluent, pleasure-seeking nobleman. However a series of visions from God changed all that. Most life-transforming of all was an experience in a tiny church in the woods near Assisi where he was worshipping on St Matthias Day, February 24, 1206. As the daily scripture was read it stood out to him like letters of gold. "As you go, preach this message: 'The Kingdom of heaven is near.' Heal the sick, raise the dead, cleanse those who have leprosy, drive out demons. Freely you have received, freely give. Do not take along any gold or silver or copper in your belts; take no bag for the journey, or extra tunic, or sandals or a staff; for the worker is worth his keep" (Matthew 10:7–10). Young Francis responded by giving away all his wealth to the poor and following Christ in poverty. Out of the counter-cultural monastic order he founded, millions of lives have been touched by the love of God. Even today both lay Protestants and Catholics, who are seeking a whole-life faith, often choose to become Third Order (or Tertiary) Franciscans following the four goals of this movement: Humility, Simplicity, Poverty and Prayer.[9]

Witness to a whole life among the suffering

Florence Nightingale's parents were wealthy and high-born. She grew up surrounded by luxury. However even as a young child Florence was stirred by compassion for the sick and afflicted. By the time she was 16 her passion had jelled. "God called me to his service – nursing." She willingly left behind the affluence, security and comfort of life in England to minister to victims of the Crimean War . . . suffering much personal hardship. Today we hail Florence Nightingale as "the lady with the lamp", the mother of the caring profession of nursing.[10] Again for her following Christ was not something she worked in around the edges of a busy professional life. Her decision led to a fundamental change in the direction of her entire life.

Witnessing to whole-life faith among ordinary Brits

From the beginning of his ministry John Wesley called very ordinary, often impoverished people to a very radical whole-life faith that slowly changed every part of their lives. Wesley had great respect for the monastic tradition and understood that we all need strong community support structures in order to follow Christ's call to radical discipleship. He instituted a system of "classes" and "bands" that became the vital core of early Methodism. In addition to Sunday worship believers would come together one night a week in small groups for personal nurture, prayer and accountability. People in these groups took time to care for one another, often pooling their meagre financial resources and sharing the good news in word and deed with their neighbours. It was through this commitment of ordinary working class people to a radical whole-life faith that the gospel spread like wild fire through English slums, mining communities and the countryside, igniting vital faith everywhere it spread.[11]

What all these models from our Christian past have in common is the conviction that the call to follow Christ was intended to transform every part of life. Not only was the direction of their lives changed, but clearly their life goals were altered as well.

Goal setting: a doorway to a whole-life faith

We all want the best that God has for us. And I believe most Christians really want to find a whole-life faith that looks more like the City of Shalom than the Boom City Mall. You have already begun the journey towards a more satisfying whole-life faith by drafting a beginning mission statement. The next step is actually to use your mission statement and the active listening you did in the last chapter to draft goals for every part of your life. Drafting goals will enable you not only to put flesh and bone on your mission statement but also to create a way of life that really begins to take on some of the authentic characteristics of the culture of God's kingdom.

Taking goal setting seriously

Richard Foster, in his classic *Celebration of Discipline*, encourages serious disciples to periodically set goals for their entire lives. He emphasizes that goal setting does not have to be "cold and calculating" like a marketing plan. Goals can enable us to more fully live out our inner faith in a way that even transforms our relationships. I am sure you know that God is interested in every aspect of our lives and wants to conform every part to the image of Christ. Setting goals can help us more authentically reflect God's character and the values of God's kingdom seven days a week.[12]

Stephen Covey in his book *First Things First* also recognizes the importance of this inner focus for our goal setting. "Goals that are connected to our inner life have the power of passion and principle," he tells us. "They're fueled by the fire within and based on 'true north' principles that create quality-of-life results."[13] The "fire within" for followers of Christ should be our desire to see God's kingdom come in our lives, communities and the world where God has placed us. And when we set goals that reflect this passion for God's kingdom everything we do will slowly be transformed. As Stephen Covey says, it is the motive for our goals that "gives us the energy to stay strong in hard moments. It gives us the strength to say 'no' because we connect with a deeper 'yes!' burning inside."[14]

One of the most important areas in which we need to find "true north" principles is in our relationship to the dominant culture that has been so influential in all of our lives. Like those first disciples we need God's help in setting goals not only for the transformation of our spiritual lives and our moral values but our cultural values too. Setting goals for every part of our lives that reflects the aspirations and values of God's kingdom will enable us to put a third leg on our discipleship stool.

When we go on our quarterly two-day prayer retreats one of the most important activities is goal setting. We start by reviewing where we have messed up in the past three months and asking God's forgiveness. Then we read our mission statement aloud and ask God to show us how we can express it in every part of our lives in the next three months and share what we are hearing. Then we intentionally express that sense of direction by setting goals for every part of our lives that reflect our sense of vocation, and we share those goals with each other. Outlined below are the headings we use in our goal setting. We hope they are helpful to you.

No. 1: setting goals for our spiritual journey

In looking back on Jesus' daily life it is obvious that he gave highest priority to intimacy with the God who called him. His entire life, including his words of hope and his acts of compassion, seemed to flow directly out of this relationship. Remarkably God invites all of us to the same kind of intimate relationship where we begin to touch the wonder and mystery of that realm which pervades our world. We will only discover who we are and who God calls us to be in that larger story as we learn to dwell deeply in the God revealed in Jesus Christ. Henri Nouwen states, "To pray is to descend with the heart, and there to stand before the face of the Lord, ever present all seeing within you."[15]

We need to learn to richly cultivate our inner life through scripture study and meditation, contemplation, silence, intercession, praise and thanksgiving. Some of the resources we have found helpful in developing spiritual disciplines are: Richard Foster, *Celebration of Discipline,* and *Prayer;* David Adam, *The Rhythm of Life;*[16] and *The Book of Common Prayer.*

This is the place we begin our goal setting process. For example, on one of our recent retreats Tom set the goal of daily time not only to read scripture but also to do an inductive study through Isaiah. The most important goal for all of us is simply to set aside and protect our time alone with God in prayer and scripture study. We encourage you to start small, with perhaps 15 minutes a day and then expand this part of your disciplines as God enables you. Find a time and a place during the day where you can get away from other distractions and be fully present to God. For us the mornings are best. For some your best time might be at lunch break or after the kids are in bed. As Richard Foster emphasizes, spending more time in prayer won't make any of us more spiritual. But it does put us in a place where God can get at us.

We encourage you to set goals not only for daily spiritual disciplines but also for areas of spiritual growth you feel God is prompting you to work on. We know people who have set goals aimed at growth in their trust in God, or to seek God's help in being more loving to those around them. We also recognize that our spiritual lives cannot be divorced from the Body of Christ. So we also suggest you set goals for protecting weekly worship as well as time for small support groups.

No. 2: setting goals for your kingdom vocation

As we read the gospels we always find Jesus in one of two places. He is either with God or with people. He didn't seem to have much time for anything else. Unfortunately these seem to be the two things we have the hardest time working into our schedules. Jesus understood that it wasn't enough to be committed to God. Our faith also requires us to be committed to the kingdom purposes of God. As a consequence, in the gospels we always find Jesus healing the broken, hugging kids and teaching his disciples about a new way of life.

Let's be clear. As mentioned earlier we don't believe scripture teaches that our jobs are automatically our kingdom vocations. But we can certainly find ways to work for God's kingdom there. The question you need to answer here is: "How do you believe God wants you to implement your mission statement in mission to others?" What is one intentional way you can seek to advance God's kingdom in your workplace, your community or through your home and family?

We suggest you reflect again on the purposes of God's kingdom and then read your mission statement aloud. In light of the ways you believe God is calling you to advance the purposes of the kingdom, what goals do you feel prompted to write? Do you sense that you should set a goal to have lunch on a regular basis with one of your work mates? Perhaps you feel inclined to do what Jerry Sittser did and set the goal of involving your kids in regular outreach to some of the forgotten people in your community. Or maybe God is encouraging you to open your home for foster kids or international students.

No. 3: setting goals for your intellectual disciplines

We find a significant difference between the reading habits of Christians in the United States compared to Britain. Believers in Britain tend to read more and work more actively to understand both their faith and the world in which God has planted them. We urge all Christians to develop a regular reading discipline. Again, for those who read very little we would suggest you start small and set incremental goals to create a basic discipline that includes a daily paper delivered to your house or a paper on the web with good international coverage like the *Independent*. We also suggest a news magazine every week. Tom's favourite is the *Economist* because it includes perspectives from both Europe and America. At least one Christian magazine like *Christianity & Renewal* or a newspaper like *The Christian Herald* is also essential. And if at all possible try to set the goal of reading a book a month . . . both serious faith-related topics and general fiction and non-fiction. An alternative goal for people of all ages is to go back to school to prepare to pursue God's call on your life. Others are taking courses to simply grow in understanding of faith and culture.

No. 4: setting goals for your relationships

Jesus' life revolved more around relationships, particularly with his disciples, than around organizations. He rarely carried all the responsibility for the ministry on his own shoulders. It was like an on-the-job apprenticeship programme in which Jesus taught his disciples to do everything he did. But they didn't just work together. We also constantly find Jesus simply enjoying time with his friends around food, wedding parties and festivals. So now we invite you to set some goals for *your* relationships. When we are on retreat we always write goals to set aside significant time for important relationships. We set goals for time not only with family and friends but also with young leaders whom God is calling us to mentor. Part of our sense of vocation is the call to hospitality. So we always carve out time for kingdom celebrations, parties with purpose and just enjoying our good friends.

Now, in light of your sense of vocation, what goals do you believe God is prompting you to draft regarding those with whom God has placed you in relationship? Do you feel you need to protect some weekly time with your family? Are there people with whom you believe God is calling you to work for reconciliation in relationship? Is God calling you to mentor a young person in your church? Is God encouraging you to create some new kingdom celebrations in your home?

No. 5: setting goals for your creative disciplines

Nowhere do we have a bigger opportunity to put a third leg on our discipleship stool than by making greater use of our creative gifts. For example, instead of simply allowing Boom City to entertain us we can use our creativity to create a range of new ways to "party our faith" seven days a week. Tom recently told some Charismatic friends in London that "they were great good fun to be with on Sunday morning during praise worship . . . but the rest of the week they were a bit of a drag." They knew he was kidding but he was making a very serious point. We Christians need to be challenged to use our creativity to bring our faith into every part of our lives . . . including how we celebrate life.

Several years ago we created a celebration called Africa Night. Our 25 dinner guests wore African or tropical attire, we played African music and enjoyed a rich African feast – spicy Ugandan ground nut stew, Ethiopian beetroot salad, couscous and African flat bread. We feasted as though we were enjoying the great Kingdom homecoming banquet. Afterwards Christine showed slides from her work on the ship up and down the west coast of Africa. We ended the evening thanking God for the rapid growth of the church throughout many countries in Africa and prayed for our neighbours struggling with hunger, malnutrition and the AIDS epidemic.

Set goals using your creative gifts in the arts, hospitality and gardening in ways that reflect the purposes and celebration of God's kingdom. Christine loves to garden and uses gardening not only as a creative outlet but also as a way to enter into the celebration of God's creation. But as part of our plan for whole-life stewardship we have also set the goal of raising 60 per cent of our vegetables in our own yard and usually have an abundance to give away.

No. 6: setting goals for your physical disciplines

Tom says "it is difficult to minister without a body." We do need to be good stewards of the bodies God has entrusted to us. As a physician Christine sees many Christians who believe their sicknesses are just an inevitable part of life. However, often their illnesses are not inevitable at all but are a result of lifestyle choices they have made. We set goals about eight years ago to create a festive low-fat diet and we do aerobic walking four to six times a week. In light of your sense of God's call on your life, set some goals for both your diet and your physical disciplines.

No. 7: setting goals for the use of your time and money

When we come back from our retreat times we not only have a new set of goals for every part of our lives, we also have a new time schedule that directly reflects these. Through our financial disciplines we have been able to get out of debt and we restrict ourselves to one credit card that we pay off every month. We are called not only to be whole-life disciples but whole-life stewards as well. In the next chapter we will explore this subject in more detail. But do consider setting some serious new goals for yourself in how you steward your time and money that more genuinely reflect the values of the kingdom rather than the seductions of Boom City. Prayerfully consider trying to free up more time or money for the work of the kingdom.

Off Ramp No. 8
An opportunity to set kingdom goals

Now it is time for you to take the next off ramp and try your hand at setting goals that begin to bring your faith and mission statement to bear on every part of your life. As we begin this goal-setting process Foster encourages us to set "realistic goals but to be willing to dream to stretch".[17] We invite you to use the dream of God's shalom future from Chapter two and your beginning mission statement from Chapter three to stretch you in some new directions. If at all possible try to take at least a mini-retreat to have significant time to work on this important process.

1. Start the goal-setting process by writing your mission statement at the top of a page in your journal along with any scripture that is particularly important for you. Also review again what you heard God saying to you through the Active Listening Process. Finally, spend some time in prayer with your spouse or by yourself praying for God's guidance.

2. Using the areas of goal setting we have just discussed, prayerfully set goals for every part of your life that both put wheels under your mission statement and more authentically reflect the values of God's kingdom.

3. Now compare the implicit goals in your life that you wrote down on off ramp 7 with those you have just drafted. What are the similarities and differences?

4. Honestly, what will it take to implement the goals you have just listed? If your goals represent major change in your life we advise you to work on implementing only one new goal at a time. When that is mastered move on to the next until you have, by God's grace and the support of family and friends, done the entire list. Share your list of goals and the other answers to these questions with your small group and ask for both prayer support and accountability as you begin this important journey towards a whole-life faith.

Goals make a difference

Carey is a woman with a mission. She feels called to empower the urban poor through helping the City Light Ministry to partner with suburban churches. Her mission statement reads: "To learn the art of loving, to practice the freedom of simplicity, to encourage the power of connectedness, to dwell in the grace of God." She told us that drafting a mission statement and then setting specific goals for every part of her life has been a godsend because she is pulled in so many different directions. She juggles being a wife and mother, a family member, friend, neighbour, home manager, mentor and member of City Light. Disciplined living has really helped her sort out her priorities.

Carey's journey to live more intentionally resulted in some fairly major life changes. For example, she and her family relocated from the inner city to the suburbs so that her life could become a better bridge connecting her suburban friends to the needs of the city. She also gave up her job for a few years to be a more vital part of the City Light Ministry. As you can imagine, her goals have often created tension with the culture around her.

Carey's sharpened sense of mission has helped bring together not only different fragments of her busy life but elements of her very diverse community too. She regularly takes her son Greg as she builds those important bridges. Greg calls her the "Robin Hood of urban missions", taking from the suburbs to give to the city.

Living on purpose ... suggestions for the journey

Learning the freedom of discipline

Earlier we described the huge victory of America's women's soccer team winning the World Cup for the first time ever. One cannot read their story in *Girls of Summer* without realizing that they would never have accomplished this achievement without two essential ingredients. First, they set goals for every part of their game, and second they imposed a rigorous discipline on themselves to achieve those goals. Every athlete, musician and scholar knows that growth isn't possible without both setting goals and then undergoing rigorous discipline to attain those goals. Remember, Paul urges us to this same kind of rigour in our race: "Let us throw off everything that hinders and the sin that so easily entangles and let us run with perseverance the race marked out for us" Hebrews 12:1b.

We see Christians of all ages who never set goals for any part of their lives or ask anything of themselves in terms of life disciplines. As a consequence there is virtually no evidence of growth in any part of their lives. They succumb easily to the pressures around them and most tragically miss the best that God has for them. To be a disciple of Jesus means to discipline every part of our lives by God's grace and through the power of the Holy Spirit, to become more like the One that we follow. Missionary statesman E. Stanley Jones suggests that disciplines need to become a "spontaneous habit" for a disciple of Jesus Christ. He adds that for a concert violinist "rules become a regularity, the laws become a liberty".[18] We find that Christians who are living on purpose and using disciplines to grow their lives also experience a new sense of liberty and freedom. They feel more in charge of their lives and are more in the groove that God has called them to.

We encourage you to take time to celebrate with your friends every single goal you implement that moves you towards a more integrated whole-life faith as though you have just won another race. When you fail to achieve a goal, like an athlete don't get discouraged but see it as a learning opportunity. With the reflection of your support group try to figure out why you missed the mark. Perhaps you need to consider another approach that is more realistic to implement your goal. Goals should be fluid, able to be adapted and changed or even replaced if necessary. But do challenge yourself to see real growth in every part of your life.

Lastly, write down the stories and adventures you experience in implementing your goals. They will help you track your progress and also keep a sense of humour when things go awry. We take an hour or two every week before we go to church to journal, pray and review how well we are succeeding in implementing our goals. We would encourage you too to find time for a weekly review of your progress. We also suggest you go on a retreat every six months to re-do your goals to keep up to date with both God's call and with changes in your life.

Remember we don't run alone

Jesus reminds all of us that we aren't alone in this race to find the best that God has for us . . . an integrated whole-life faith with a difference. Remember Jesus' important assurance, "Come to me, all you who are weary and burdened, and I will give you rest." Christ continues. "Take my yoke upon you and learn from me, for I am gentle and humble in heart, and you will find rest for your souls. For my yoke is easy and my burden is light" (Matthew 11:28–30).

Dallas Willard says, "The secret of the easy yoke, then, is to learn from Christ how to live our total lives, how to invest all our time and our energies of mind and body as he did. We must learn how to follow his preparations, the disciplines for life in God's rule that enabled him to receive his Father's constant and effective support while doing his will."[19] We find when we help people set new goals they tell us that they often don't have the time to implement them. In the next chapter we will attempt to respond to this issue. We will help you reinvent your timestyle and lifestyle not only to free up more time and resources to implement your new goals but also to create a more festive way of life that begins to reflect a little more of the character values of the new shalom future of God rather than the addictions of modern culture.

Notes

1. Naomi B. Stone, Ed. Thomas Merton, *A Vow of Conversation*, Journal 1964–65, Basingstoke, UK, The Lamp Press, 1988, p. 71.

2. Rodney Clapp, *A Peculiar People*, Downers Grove: InterVarsity Press, 1996, p. 89.

3. David J. Bosch, *Transforming Mission*, Maryknoll, NY: Orbis, 1991, p. 48.

4. *Missional Church*, ed. Darrell L. Guder, Grand Rapids: Eerdmanns, 1998, p. 224.

5. Clapp, p. 88.

6. Wayne Meeks, *The Origin of Christian Morality*, New Haven: Yale University Press, 1993, p. 12.

7. Michael Mitton, *Restoring the Woven Cord*, London: Darton Longman & Todd, 1995, p. 124.

8. Esther de Waal, *The Celtic Way of Prayer*, New York: Doubleday, 1997, p. 30.

9. John R. H. Moorman, *St Francis of Assisi*, London: SPCK, 1963, p. 19.

10. For an account of Florence Nightingale's life and work see *Florence Nightingale; The Lady of the Lamp*, Basil Miller, Grand Rapids: Zondervan, 1947.

11. Howard Snyder, *The Radical Wesley*, Downers Grove: InterVarsity Press, 1980, pp. 53–64.

12. Richard Foster, *Celebration of Discipline*, San Francisco: Harper & Row, 1978, pp. 94–95. (UK edition: Hodder & Stoughton).

13. Stephen R. Covey, A. Roger Merrill and Rebecca R. Merrill, *First Things First*, New York: Simon & Schuster, 1994, p. 140.

14. Covey, et al., p. 142.

15. Henri Nouwen, *The Way of the Heart*, New York: Ballantine, 1985, p. 59.

16. David Adam, *The Rhythm of Life: Celtic Daily Prayer*, Harrisburg, PA: Morehouse Publishing, 1996.

17. Richard Foster, *Celebration of Discipline*, San Francisco: Harper & Row, 1978, pp. 94–95.
18. E. Stanley Jones, *The Way*, Nashville: Abingdon-Cokesbury, 1955, p. 231.
19. Dallas Willard, *The Spirit of the Disciplines*, San Francisco: Harper & Row, 1988, p. 9.

5 Living on Purpose: Creating a Way of Life You Can Love

This day is your love gift to me,
This dawn I take it from your hand.
Make me busy in your service throughout its hours,
Yet not so busy that I cannot sing a happy song
And may the south wind blow its tenderness through my heart,
So that I bear myself gently towards all.
And may the sunshine of it pass into my thoughts,
So that each shall be a picture of your thoughts, noble & right.

Author unknown

"Do you have any idea what it is like to live in Dallas, Texas with the Cowboys?" asked Tony Evans, a popular American evangelist. He was speaking to a packed-out auditorium at the Christian Community Development Association Conference in 1998 about one of the top American football teams. He said "If you live in Dallas, Texas you are obsessed with the Cowboys. You can hardly go through a day at work without someone mentioning the Cowboys . . . discussing who is injured and who is going to play next Sunday. In fact the Dallas Cowboys control the entire atmosphere of the city.

"The King of Kings and Lord of Lords doesn't just want an hour or two of your time during the week either. God wants to be the one to permeate the atmosphere of your entire life instead of the Cowboys." Tony wasn't putting down the Dallas Cowboys. He is reminding us that if we really want to find the best for our lives we won't find it through a "Sunday go to meeting faith" where our sports, work, shopping or anything else sets the priorities and rhythm for our daily life.

Finding the focus

You are well on your way to finding God's best for your life. In Chapter three you hopefully drafted a beginning mission statement to put God's purposes first. In the last chapter you outlined goals to begin the journey towards a whole-life faith. In this chapter we want to enable you to reinvent your timestyle and lifestyle to create a liturgy of life you can love, and free up more time and resources to invest in the advance of God's kingdom. In fact most people find it isn't really possible to seriously implement either their mission statements or their goals without making some major changes in how they steward their time and their resources.

In this chapter we will take a good hard look at what constitutes a biblical view of stewardship of our time and money. We will also outline some imaginative, practical ways you can create a liturgy of life that reflects the rhythms of the City of Shalom instead of the rip tides of Boom City. Let's take a quick look back at how the culture has defined the rhythm of our lives.

A living blur ...

For too many of us life has become little more than a living blur. If we have any kind of liturgy of life it is likely to be shaped more by the *Today* programme, the Stock Exchange reports, "fly on the wall" television and our e-mail routines than anything that comes from our Christian faith. But we find people everywhere who want to take back their lives. They not only want to overcome their "hurry sickness", their stress and their 24/7 on-line lifestyles but they want to rediscover an easier rhythm that is more in touch with both the creation and their Creator. They also want to be more responsible stewards of both their time and their money.

Dorothy Bass writes, "Fueled by a global marketplace that leaps across time zones in a single bound, a new pattern of time is emerging, one that moves to a digital beat that has no regard for night nor day [never mind Sunday or Monday, winter or summer]. The Internet is both its emblem and its foundation, and e-mailers and Web surfers have been among the first to learn its paces."[1] We are paying high costs in our lives and churches for our blurred existence.

Counting the high costs of disconnected living

Costs to the vitality of our faith

Many of us find we are out of sync with the created order, our own natural rhythms and even our spiritual core. As we saw in Chapter one we are paying a very high price in our health, our relationships and our personal values for this epidemic of hurry sickness. Let's look at some of the specific costs to the vitality of our faith and the viability of the church as we race into the 21st century.

A number of Bible societies report that daily Bible reading among Christians has declined rapidly in recent years in spite of an explosion of print and on-line biblical resources. Alarming numbers of Christian leaders in local churches tell us they are so pressed for time that their only prayer is with the pastor before the Sunday morning service. Believers tell us the only rituals of faith they celebrate are Sunday morning worship plus Christmas and Easter. And the apostles of Boom City are even trying to transform those two Christian holy days into celebrations of consumption. Tragically they have largely succeeded. In fact when we asked people in a church in Sheffield "What constitutes the primary liturgy of your lives?" one woman candidly responded "The after-Christmas, pre-Easter and mid-summer sales!" What comprises the liturgy of your life?

Costs to the viability of the church and its mission

As the global consumer culture increasingly gobbles up our time and resources it is not only undermining the vitality of the church but also undercutting our support for missions around the world. We are witnessing the slow but serious haemorrhaging of time and money invested in the work of the church. Let's look at some of the serious patterns of decline in church attendance and giving patterns.

In the US some megachurches, Black and Hispanic churches and a few evangelical and Pentecostal denominations are experiencing growth, but unfortunately that's not the whole story. Virtually all mainline denominations are greying much more rapidly than the population and are experiencing a serious decline in attendance. As a consequence, though few talk about it, the Christian presence in American society is actually shrinking because population growth is outstripping the very slow rate of growth of the church. Empty Tomb research reports that Christians in the US who constituted 45 per cent of the population in 1968, declined to 39 per cent in 1997 and are still losing ground.[2] The missing generation we are losing in record numbers, according to Barna Research, is the under 35s. We aren't doing a very good job of keeping our own young or reaching out to the unchurched young.

In Britain too there is some growth amongst evangelical churches but the established old-line denominations such as Methodist and Anglican are greying and declining more rapidly than others are able to grow the church. As a consequence adult church attendance has declined from 10.2 per cent of the population attending church weekly in 1980 to 7.5 per cent in 2000.[3] The age group least likely to attend church are the 20-year-olds.[4]

In both Britain and the US, in spite of a decade of economic boom times Christians are actually giving not only less of their time to things of faith but less of their money too. In the US "Per member giving as a percentage of income declined from 3.10 % in 1968 to 2.52% in 1998, a decline of 19% . . ."[5] In denominational giving to charity we are witnessing an even more serious decline. In 1968 21 per cent of every dollar went to charity. By 1998 that had declined to 16 per cent, a 40 per cent decline. Researchers at Empty Tomb predict that if this trend continues charitable giving will reach zero by 2043.[6] In

Off Ramp No. 9

Checking out rhythms of life and stewardship of life

 It is time to take another break and find out what is happening in both the stewardship of your congregation and the rhythms of Christian life.

1. Ask your pastor or church treasurer if participation in church activities and giving has increased or decreased in the past five years. Specifically ask what percentage is given to missions outreach both locally and globally. Has that increased or decreased? Take the information you are given and draw a simple chart that shows the stewardship trends in your church.

2. Sample a few people in your church and ask them to describe how their faith shapes the rhythms of their lives and what the competing pressures are in terms of everything from daily devotions, to weekly worship to the celebration of Christian holy days.

3. Now it's your turn. Describe your pattern of Christian observances in the past year and list the factors in your life which most directly compete with those observances.

4. Identify specific ways you might alter some of those pressures to more faithfully maintain your Christian observances as well as being a more faithful steward of your time and your money. Share with your group or your friend and pray for God's help.

Britain, evidence shows that from 1974 to 1994 there was a steady decline in the proportion of British households giving to charity, but this trend has stabilized in the last few years.[7]

Remember that between 2010 and 2030 the Baby Boomers will all retire, which means their church giving will probably begin to decline sharply too. The under 35s who do stay with the church will be less numerous with less money left to support the church for two reasons. First, numbers of them are carrying much more school debt than their elders. Second, while few from our generation ever paid much over 20 per cent of our incomes for rent or mortgage we are finding that an astonishing number of young people in both the US and Britain today are spending over 50 per cent. If the declining attendance and giving patterns continue then there is a serious possibility we could see the post World War II missions boom go into serious decline by 2020.

Identifying the causes of our competing priorities

I am sure most of us are deeply concerned by this serious decline in the amount of time and money we are investing in our faith, the church and its mission. We should be concerned. But what are the causes? Why has our *per capita* giving declined over the past four decades while our incomes have increased? Why do we seem to have less time left over for prayer, church and service? Why does our faith seem to have so little impact on the rhythm of our lives?

Part of the answer, as we have already discussed, is that our faith is so seriously disconnected from our regular lives. Consequently as we have seen many of us have allowed the Boom City Mall instead of our faith to define what is important and of value. Another serious problem is that the church has seldom provided any forums where Christians can get help in developing biblical criteria to use in stewarding their time and money. Do you know of any churches that provide forums:

1. Where Christians who are offered a promotion that increases their work hours from 40 to 60 hours a week can discuss all the costs to family and faith?
2. Where new parents can think ahead about the best activities for their kids and how much they will cost?
3. Where Christians can find practical, biblical help in the stewardship of busy lives and tight resources?

We have found very few. Not surprisingly since the church isn't where these decisions are made, things of faith keep winding up at the bottom of most people's lists. No wonder the church is losing ground.

Flawed models of stewardship

We believe there is another answer to the question, "Why are our levels of involvement and investment in the mission of God's kingdom in such serious decline?" The church at large is working from some seriously flawed notions of what biblical stewardship looks like. First, most of the stewardship materials we see tend to uncritically accept as a given the affluent lifestyle and workplace demands of modern culture and simply try to help believers be good stewards of whatever time or money is left over. This culturally accommodated approach to Christian stewardship asks very little of disciples of Jesus and often settles for even less.

In addition we believe we are working from three flawed models of stewardship that also help explain our declining levels of giving and involvement:

1. Myth of the blessing model
2. Myth of the tithe model
3. Myth of the downscaling model

In contrast to these three models we will present a fourth possibility . . . a whole-life stewardship model. We sincerely believe that those who are willing to give this fourth model a try will find a way of life with an exciting difference.

Myth of the blessing model

One of the most popular myths regarding Christian stewardship is the blessing model. This view is particularly popular with those who subscribe to the "Prosperity Gospel", as well as a number of charismatic groups, and though it is more common in the US, we find growing numbers of evangelical and charismatic Christians in Britain, Australia and New Zealand who adhere to this model. It also has growing influence in many parts of Africa, the Middle East and Asia.

In this model believers are encouraged to prove God's faithfulness by asking for a broad range of personal blessings. They are encouraged to trust God to give them wealth, success and status beyond their wildest dreams . . . to prove God's faithfulness. As an expression of their faith they are challenged to give generously to the church even before their prayers are answered. We have a large church in Seattle devoted to this kind of prosperity gospel where the pastoral staff live lavishly off these "faith" contributions, displaying to their congregation the big payoff for trusting God.

There are a number of problems with this mythical model of blessing stewardship. Problem number one is that it starts with me and my desires. It really is all about seeking a blessing for me rather than discovering how God can use my life to be a blessing to God and others. Think about it. Nowhere in the New Testament do we find those earliest Christian leaders praying prayers of faith for their own needs, let alone asking God for abundant wealth and success. We never find Paul praying for more lavish accommodations at his next stop or Peter praying that the family fishing business will double its income in the coming year. Doesn't God care about us personally? Absolutely! But we can't imagine a God of compassion wanting to bless us with a new Lexus while our friends in Haiti are struggling to keep their kids fed. Can you?

The second problem with this model is that it baptizes greed and self-interest instead of challenging them. In fact it buys fully into the Boom City definition of the good life as the pursuit of economic upscaling, status and consumption . . . and Jesus too, as though it all goes together. And the proponents of this view would have us believe that acquiring all the goodies in the Boom City Mall is what Jesus meant by the "abundant life". The third problem is that, for all the proof texts out of Proverbs, this model simply isn't biblical. While in the vision of the shalom future God clearly cares about every part of our lives including our physical needs, God's special concern is for the physical needs of the most vulnerable in our midst. Jesus repeatedly challenged his followers to sell their possessions to help the needy in their midst. Somehow the advocates for this view have conveniently forgotten that Jesus doesn't call us to seek life but rather to lose it.

If you want to find the actual origins of the prosperity gospel you won't find it in the teachings of Jesus. Check out the writings of one of America's founding fathers, who happened to be a deist . . . one Ben Franklin. Ben insisted that the goal of life wasn't virtue, as Christians in his day believed, but rather prosperity and success. He declared that wealth, success and status are the real goals of life. Virtue is simply the means to achieve those goals. Sound familiar?

I realize many people in all kinds of churches are quite taken by the book *The Prayer of Jabez*, which encourages the readers to pray for blessings. We need to be encouraged by anything that persuades Christians to pray. But while Jabez, in a different time and place, did indeed ask God to bless him and expand his territories, we have seen over and over that the scripture as a whole calls us to a way of life, like the One we follow, in which we can be instruments of God's blessing to others.

Myth of the tithe model

By far the most prominent model of stewardship today is the tithe model. In fact virtually all the materials that call Christians to serious stewardship work from a 10 per cent (tithe) viewpoint. While we fully appreciate the Old Testament origins of the tithe a growing numbers of New Testament theologians including Craig Blomberg, at Denver Seminary, say there is absolutely no New Testament support for setting the bar at giving 10 per cent of our income to the church.[8] Any thoughtful read of the New Testament shows that Jesus and that first community raised the bar on what it means to be a faithful steward, just as Jesus did on a number of other ethical issues.

Please understand, it would be great if the church could actually persuade their people to give 10 per cent of their income. As we have seen *per capita* giving for the American church has actually declined from 3.10 per cent in 1968 to 2.52 per cent in 1998.[9] Clearly this is an important time to re-examine New

Testament teachings on what kind of stewardship Jesus calls us to.

One major problem with tithe stewardship is that as soon as a person gives a certain percentage of their income they often feel they are off the hook. What they do with the rest is pretty much their own business. We are very concerned that the tithe model tends to cause many of us to fragment our sense of responsibility, and that contributes to our disconnected faith. Take a serious look at some of the more visible models in the New Testament. When Zaccheus chose to follow Christ he gave half to the poor and offered to pay back four times any that he defrauded. The rich young ruler was challenged to sell all his possessions and to follow Jesus. And that wasn't a salvation quiz. Jesus really meant it. In Jerusalem church members sold their possessions to help their needier sisters and brothers. Of course not everyone gave away all their resources, but it seems evident that following Christ was seen as a whole-life proposition. Plus the decision to become a disciple of this Jesus seemed to have a more radical impact on how those believers stewarded their resources than we typically see today. Jacques Ellul in *Money and Power* argues that we also need to take Mammon, which Jesus warned us about, much more seriously. He states it is a spiritual power that will dominate our lives if we don't deal with it.[10]

Walter Pilgrim, in his very provocative book *Good News to the Poor: Wealth and Poverty in Luke/Acts*, believes that Jesus raised the standard much higher than many of us are willing to acknowledge. Jesus said, "Do not be afraid, little flock, for your Father has been pleased to give you the kingdom. Sell your possessions and give to the poor. Provide purses for yourselves that will not wear out, a treasure in heaven that will not be exhausted, where no thief comes near and no moth destroys. For where your treasure is there your heart will be also" (Luke 12:32–34).

Pilgrim writes, "At stake in this passage is the life and death matter of inheriting the kingdom of becoming 'rich toward God', of realizing one's life doesn't consist in the abundance of possessions, of seeking the kingdom and trusting God for our daily needs, of looking inward to discern whether the treasures in one's heart lies in God or mammon. Therefore the meaning of the command to sell one's possessions . . . is a command to sell all in the service of the kingdom and the discipleship of Jesus."[11]

Blomberg, reflecting on the fact that the New Testament does indeed raise the bar on what it means to be a faithful steward, writes "Those who are at least reasonably well off should give considerably more than a tenth of their gross income to God's work."[12] Ron Sider has long challenged believers to consider giving a graduated tithe as God prospers them. There are a number of people in our churches today who could double or triple their tithe and not change their lifestyle one iota.

Myth of the downscaling model

Ron Sider's book, *Rich Christians in an Age of Hunger*, challenged many of us back in the late seventies to re-think our lifestyle priorities. It called Christians everywhere to downscale our lifestyles, "to live simply that others might simply live".[13] In response to the challenge of that book and several others virtually every mainline denomination in the late seventies developed stewardship educational materials on how to simplify our lifestyles. But that emphasis very quickly ran out of gas. Then in the nineties ardent environmentalists called their adherents to a similar "downshifting model" of lifestyle change.

We believe that the downscaling movement is right to remind us that there is no such thing as "private" lifestyle choices. We do indeed live in an interdependent, interconnected world in which our decisions often impact the lives of people half a world away. Conversely if we can find creative ways to free up some of our time and money and invest it to help those at the margins the impacts can be great. Downscalers are also right in challenging us to ask the absolutely essential question for Christian stewards: "How much is enough?" How much of our resources do we really need to spend on our own wardrobe, transportation, housing or recreation when believers in other parts of the world have difficulty just feeding their families?

Where we believe downscalers have it wrong is that we don't believe we are called simply to do a downscaled version of the Western dream. We believe we are called to biblically reinvent it . . . to create a more festive way of life where we not only cut back – but we also add *celebration* to our lives in a way that reflects the jubilation of God's new order.

A biblical model of whole-life stewardship

A biblical view of stewardship isn't about seeking our own blessing, sharing 10 per cent of our income or even doing a simplified version of the Western dream. It is about turning our back on the land of illusions and joining others in seeking to flesh out something of God's shalom future. Whole-life stewardship is the biblical call to intentionally steward our entire lives in a way that:

1. More authentically reflects the values and rhythms of God's new order
2. Frees up more of both time and money to be invested in advancing this new order

Scott Rodin, in his important book *Stewards in the Kingdom*, declares, "The coming of the kingdom of God is ushering into existence a fundamentally new sense of what is real and what is counterfeit. The claims of Jesus call us to see God, the world and ourselves through an entirely new set of lenses . . . Money, fame, health, security, all the *real* things are facades . . . The incarnation announced . . . the coming of a new reality . . . that calls us to committed engagement with the world."[14] We are invited to leave the facades and illusions of wealth, status and upscaling behind and discover through an incarnational whole-life faith what is real.

What we propose is that we journey towards incarnational whole-life stewardship by asking from scripture what we explored in Chapter two: "What are God's purposes for a people and a world?" Once we have reminded ourselves of

God's destination then we simply ask "how might God want to use my mustard seed both to herald the celebration and to advance God's transforming purposes in our needy world?"

There is no dualism between sacred and secular here. God delights in taking the ordinary stuff of life and making it sacred. "For Christianity does not destroy what is natural but ennobles it. To turn water into wine, what is common into what is holy is indeed the glory of Christianity. It is the continuous theme of the Gospels that God transforms what is available: The five loaves and two fishes, the Passover bread, and the wine, the water at the marriage feast. It is as if he demands from men and from nature all that they can manage and then takes it and changes it and uses it for his purposes."[15] As we make God's story our story, somehow our stories are transformed into God's story. Then everything in our lives takes on a new sense of significance beyond anything we imagined possible. Amazingly our ordinary broken lives, joined with others, can become the fragrant gardens of God's new order.

Whole-life stewardship is premised on the strong biblical assertion of Psalm 104 "that the earth is the Lord's and the fullness thereof". In the story of the faithful manager Jesus also makes it very clear that we are not owners but only stewards of what God has provided (Luke 12: 41–48). Listen to Jesus' instructions for whole-life disciples that we cited before, "Do not be afraid, little flock, for your Father has been pleased to give you the kingdom. Sell your possessions and give to the poor. Provide purses for yourselves that will not wear out, a treasure in heaven that will not be exhausted . . . For where your treasure is, there your heart will be also" (Luke 12:32–34). Over and over one of the primary evidences that a person had chosen to follow Christ was the dramatic difference it made in how they stewarded their lives and resources.

Whole-life stewardship in action

This whole-life stewardship modelled in the New Testament reflected the biblical principle that all of our lives and possessions belong to God. Today many Christians would agree that everything they have belongs to God but their role is to passively sit back and enjoy it for God . . . until God gives them a divine revelation that he intends to use them in other ways. We believe disciples are not called to wait for a lightning bolt but to actively reinvent our use of time and money in a way that reflects God's purposes. Donald Kraybill, in his provocative book, *The Upside Down Kingdom,* urges that "faithful stewards are frugal when calculating their own needs and generous in responding to the needs of others."[16] We need to ask: "What percentage of our time and money do we really need to spend on meeting our essential needs . . . not all our wants?" If we candidly answer that question I suspect we will be surprised at how much of our lives could be available for investment in God's great drama. Let's put whole-life stewardship into action!

Freeing up time to put first things first

Take out a copy of your weekly time schedule. Carefully and prayerfully review all your time commitments in light of your mission statement and your goals. Be ruthless. Cut out everything that doesn't reflect what you believe is God's call on your life. It might mean quitting a part-time job and doing with a little less spending money to take part of your life back. It may mean cutting back the time you spend watching TV, trips to the mall, some of your kid's activities or even getting off a committee at church. Cut every single area possible.

Once you have actually freed up some time resist the urge to fill it immediately with more activity. Take a few weeks and simply savour your free time. Get spontaneous. Go for a walk with your spouse or a friend. Take your kids or somebody else's kids to the zoo. Or go on an outing to a place that reconnects you to the beauty of God's creation. Then after you have established an easier rhythm prayerfully ask God "If I seriously attempted to implement my mission statement and goals how might I reinvent my time schedule?"

Freeing up money and other resources to put first things first

Look over your physical assets and budget in light of your mission statement and goals. How could you be a better steward of what God has entrusted to you? How might you seriously reduce your debt to increase your flexibility? Would it help to find professional help to effectively reduce your financial pressures? One young man actually freezes his only credit card in a block of ice to protect himself from impulse buying. How much do you really need to spend on wardrobe, transportation, entertainment, holidays and housing? Now cut back any area of your budget that seems inconsistent with your sense of calling. Again, don't immediately spend any money or other resources you release, just savour the reduced sense of pressure. Many people find if they reduce their lifestyle costs they can actually free up more time to invest in things that really matter. Prayerfully ask God "If I really decided to implement my mission statement and my goals how might it change my budget and stewardship of the other resources God has entrusted to me?"

Four hundred and fifty Americans who fall in the top 5 per cent of earners have started a Responsible Wealth Campaign to use their wealth more responsibly and to work for a more just economy.[17] All of us need to work for a more just economy and one way is to consider ethical investing to use our resources to advance God's kingdom in those groups that are empowering the poor and caring for creation. Let us share some examples of people who reinvented their timestyles and lifestyles to put first things first and the difference it has made for them.

Celebrating putting first things first

A family in Seattle changed their timestyle to release two hours a week to go to a nursing home where their two primary-aged kids read to seniors who didn't have many visitors. An older couple in Denver told Tom that after reading his book, *The Mustard Seed Conspiracy*, they sold their huge home and bought a smaller place. They felt God challenged them to use the profits to provide down payments to buy homes for two young couples in their church who are involved in urban ministry so they can reduce their lifestyle costs and not have to raise so much support.

Don has two young sons he planned to sign up for Little League baseball in Seattle. Then he discovered that other kids in his multiracial neighbourhood also wanted to play baseball but didn't have the money to join the children's Little League team. So Don decided to use his time to start an informal baseball game that didn't cost money so that both his sons and the other kids in his neighbourhood could play and have fun. The older kids taught the younger kids and they all learned to play together. As you can imagine this necessitated a major time commitment for Don but he told us that there is no question in his mind that the decision he made lines up with what he felt Jesus might have done.

Thirty young men at Warehouse, a youth church in Chichester, made another whole-life stewardship decision. They pledged to work no more than 25 hours a week for money so that they could have significant time to work with at-risk kids. Of course they have had to reduce their standard of living in order to pursue their sense of God's call on their life but again, they feel that is a small price to pay for the joy of doing what they feel Jesus would have done. Reinventing your time-style not only means you have more to share with others but it means you have the opportunity to create a way of life you will truly love.

Creating a way of life you can love

Partying the kingdom 24/7

We believe that one of the greatest weapons we can utilize to counter the seductions of Boom City is to create festivities and rituals for our lives that flow directly from our faith. We are constantly finding new ways to party our faith. As Christians we enjoy celebrating all the Jewish celebration feasts like the Feast of Booths, complete with Jewish folk dancing. But we also experiment with new ways to party the different biblical images of the kingdom of God – as Jubilee, as a lost treasure, as an international banquet, as a great homecoming celebration or a wedding feast. If you were going to bring the biblical imagery of the coming of the bridegroom and the wedding feast of God to life would you have a procession, an exchange of vows, a reception? We urge you to begin this journey to discover a way of life you can love by getting together with your children or your friends and planning a party that brings some aspect of your faith to life with great festivity.

Creating life rituals and celebrating life milestones

We encourage singles, couples and families with kids to create new rituals and new ways to celebrate the milestones of our lives. On the *Anastasis* a Christian version of the Jewish rite of passage for young people entering adulthood was created. Teresa Hill's Bat Mitzvah was held not long after Christine joined the ship in Greece. Her ceremony was set up around a special meal organized by her family and attended by the whole community. She had spent weeks preparing for this special occasion, reading books, memorizing scripture and learning about the responsibilities of being an adult in our community. A seven-candle menorah specially crafted by the welding department formed the focus of the ritual. Teresa's face glowed as she lit the final candle on the menorah and shared her testimony and community leaders prayed for her.

Graham and Treena Kerr have started the Seventh Chair Dinner Club. They recommend inviting your friends in for a meal that represents another part of the world with all the festivity and extras. Then you can invite an extra guest who is seldom invited out to fill the Seventh Chair or estimate the costs of one serving and donate that amount to a local food co-operative for the poor.

Michael and Mary Reeves decided to celebrate their 25th wedding with a difference. They invited all their friends and family who had stood alongside them in good times and in hard times over the 25 years. Seventy people showed up at a hotel in Grapevine, Texas for the celebration. Michael and Mary hosted their friends at a lovely banquet in which their sons stood with them as they renewed their vows. Mary said this coming together of family and friends was for her "a taste of what heaven would be like".

McNair Wilson, co-founder of Imaginuity Unlimited, found a particularly creative way to celebrate the milestone of his 40th birthday. He talked the managers of the Coliseum, a football stadium in Southern California, into renting him the 40-yard line at a very reasonable price for one evening. On a warm evening with the lights blazing, tables were set up, laden with food, on the 40-yard line, and fifty of McNair's friends celebrated his creative life and his vital faith.

We just celebrated Christine's 50th birthday but we did it more conventionally in our own home. For Christine the celebration really connected to the biblical theme of Jubilee, which of course was a preview of the coming of God's kingdom. Tom arranged for three friends who had served with her on the *Anastasis* to fly to Seattle to join in remembering their days of life and mission together in Africa, Asia and Latin America. Our dining room wall was festooned with pictures of those days and people reminisced with fun and laughter. A friend from our church, Coe Hutchison, prayed a prayer of dedication for our lives for the next 50 years. Not only do we have the possibility of creating new rituals and celebrating new milestones, we also have the possibility of creating a liturgy of life that flows from the rhythms of faith instead of the rat race of Boom City.

Looking back on a liturgy of faith

We find that most Christians have little idea how to work from the inspiration of their faith to create a new rhythm for their lives instead of simply trying to survive the stress-race. If you have successfully freed up some time in your schedule it will make it even easier to create a rhythm for your life that is renewing instead of exhausting. Let's take a quick look back on how vital faith seems to have shaped the rhythm of life of for many who went before us. The history of Judeo-Christian faith at its best is the history of a faith that both set the pace of life and defined the celebration of life.

A rhythm of Sabbath

From the opening act of this drama Yahweh called the Jews not only to religious fidelity and moral integrity, but to a new rhythm of life that was very different from that of their neighbours. That new rhythm began with a new word . . . Sabbath. The Sabbath was meant to be both a day of rest and of remembrance. "Therefore the Lord blessed the Sabbath day and made it holy" (Exodus 20:11). In Deuteronomy it was rooted in the remembrance of the Israelites' liberation from slavery in Egypt (Deuteronomy 5:14, 15). To this day observant Jews all over the world close the work week and celebrate Sabbath peace, *Shabbat Shalom*.[18]

Jesus' life was permeated by the Jewish sense of the "holiness of time". The rhythm of his life was established not only by the Sabbath but also by his participation, with his disciples, in the Jewish celebrations that punctuated the year. He created a very celebrative life of feasting and hospitality with his friends and followers that anticipated the great homecoming celebration of God's new order. Tom Wright reminds us that "wherever Jesus went, there seemed to be a celebration; the tradition of festive meals at which Jesus welcomed all and sundry. . . ." Wright added "The meals spoke powerfully about Jesus' vision of the kingdom . . ."[19]

A rhythm of life in our Christian past

When the Roman persecutions ended, a few Christian leaders expressed concern that without the "discipline" of persecution believers were beginning to succumb to the seductions and comforts of secular Roman culture. In response the Desert Fathers created the beginnings of the monastic movement in an effort both to bring a discipline back to life and to create a rhythm that flowed authentically from their faith. The monastic impulses of the Desert Fathers spread all over Europe including the British Isles and the emerging Celtic church.

Esther de Waal recounts in *The Celtic Way of Prayer,* "Early Celtic Christianity was above all monastic. People learned their religious beliefs and practices from the monastic communities with the monastic ideal of continual prayer. The spirituality of ordinary lay people was a monastic spirituality; ordinary lay people expected to pray the daily offices, which means, of course, essentially to follow a liturgical life shaped by a regular, ordered rhythm – yearly, seasonal, daily."[20] In the Middle Ages too the church bells beckoned the people to prayer and worship throughout the day, providing a sacred focus for the rhythm and pattern of the whole day. You can still find believers, not just in religious orders, but throughout society, whose faith shapes the rhythms of life.

Creating a liturgy of life you can love

Celebrating the Sabbath

Finding the best God has for us begins by rediscovering God's gift to the Jews . . . the sacredness of time. And our journey begins with not only rediscovering the gift of the Sabbath but of a new rhythm of life shaped not just by the pressures of work, home and Internet but by the calendar of the church year as well. Changing our timestyles to receive the Sabbath ". . . means joining in the song of creation," Dorothy Bass urges, "which renews our love for the earth and our gratitude for the blessings God grants through it. Receiving *this* day means joining in a worldwide song of liberation . . . No other days can be the same after this one."[21] She is right. Start your new liturgy of life by carving out time for a Sabbath for renewal of your life and spirit.

We are seeking ways to protect a Sabbath day. Our most successful Sabbath ritual is setting aside two hours on Sunday morning to journal about what God has taught us in the past week and what God is calling us to in the week ahead. This has become one of our very best times of sharing, prayer and reflection. Start small with a two-hour Sabbath after church or on the day which provides the greatest freedom for you . . . not as a legal duty but as a time of quiet reflection, meditation and recreation. Then as God enables you try to grow it into a full day and see how it begins to alter the rhythm of your entire week.

Recently students at Seattle Pacific University's Central Dormitory called a seven-day Sabbath fast from all TV, MTV, video games, on-line chat rooms, e-mail and web surfing. During the week they created alternative activities including a face-to-face chat room. Students said they really enjoyed having more time to actually get to know the people they lived with.

Eugene Peterson, a Presbyterian minister and his wife, keep their Sabbath on Monday. In all kinds of weather they drive into the country, read and reflect on a Psalm together and then hike for several hours, communing with the Creator and the creation. Finally they spend a quiet evening of reflection at home.[22] Marva Dawn states "Sabbath keeping is the very thing our technological world needs. Instead of society's criterion of efficiency, keeping the Sabbath offers the will and purposes of God as the ultimate criteria."[23]

Celebrating the church calendar

Neither Tom nor Christine grew up in a liturgical church but in the past ten years both have discovered the gift of following the rhythm of the Christian calendar. Donna Crow Fletcher, also from a non-liturgical background, relishes this gift too, "Following the Christian calendar is a whole new way of keeping track of time. It is living every day in relationship to the life of Christ as he lived on earth."[24] It really is a new way to journey through our days with Christ.

Celebrating Advent

Time in the church calendar is governed by the life, death and resurrection of Jesus Christ rather than by the rhythms of our frenetic culture. It begins with the season of Advent . . . a time to watch and wait. We are both Christmas people, and the discovery of Advent has dramatically expanded our appreciation of the advent of Christ, extending it from a single day to four weeks of scripture reading, meditation, and prayer complete with daily lighting of our Advent candles. Our journey through Advent begins with a time of reflection on the broken state of our world, our own struggling places and our desperate need for a saviour. Then our focus shifts to a time of anticipation not only for the coming of a Saviour but of the shalom future of God when the broken lives and crushed spirits will all be made new. By the time Christmas morning arrives we are brimming with hope and anticipation.

When Steve and Cheryl Hayner's two eldest were preschoolers they created a new family ritual by telling them the story of God's coming to the children of Israel. The children painted pictures reflecting their impressions of each segment of the story. Over the four weeks of Advent the entire story unfolded in colourful pictures that covered the walls. On Christmas Eve the Hayner family celebrated a birthday party for Jesus and exchanged gifts. On Christmas day they were involved in giving Christmas to those who had no family to celebrate with.

In Australia Christmas comes during the long hot days of summer so Christine was overwhelmed by her first winter visit to Norway on the eve of Epiphany during the Festival of Lights. Lights adorned the trees and hung in windows, illuminating the dark Scandinavian winter. She had never understood so powerfully the imagery of light breaking into darkness. Epiphany begins 12 days after Christmas and celebrates the light of Christ coming into the world.

Celebrating Lent

Stan Thornburg, a quirky friend of ours, announced, "I decided to give up self-denial for Lent this year!" When many of us think of Lent the first thing that comes up on our screen is "self-denial". But the Lenten season isn't just about self-denial, it is period of preparation for the glorious celebration of Palm Sunday and the Feast of Easter Sunday. Robert Webber points out "when we spend six and a half weeks of Lent preparing our hearts for the risen Christ 'Easter becomes a genuine experience of resurrection.'"[25]

It is impossible to journey with Jesus towards Jerusalem without reflecting on our own lives and faithfulness as his followers. Interestingly, the concept of spring cleaning emerged from the Lenten tradition. This was traditionally the time of year when one "cleaned house" first spiritually and then practically as well. As Gertrud Mueller Nelson expresses it, "I think that spring house cleaning was an old way of introspecting. We clean house, inside and outside. We let in the fresh air, shake out the bedspreads, clean out the cupboards. We collect all the inner useless accumulations of our lifestyles and contribute them to the dust and ashes that we take up again on Ash Wednesday."[26]

We encourage people to try our simple Lenten discipline. We read the Gospel scriptures about Christ's journey towards Jerusalem then invite the Holy Spirit to help us identify those places in our lives that need to experience crucifixion and resurrection. We do encourage those who are able to fast a bit and consider a little self-denial from the addictions or distractions of Boom City . . . from on-line shopping to video games.

One of Christine's most vivid images of Easter was in Greece where this feast is the focal point for Christians. The fragrant aroma of lamb wafted towards her as she walked along a dusty street in Elevsis. *Ella, ella!* (Come, come!) people called, beckoning her in to join the magnificent Easter feast. Shouts of *Christo anasti* (Christ is risen) brought the response *Allythos anasti* (He is risen indeed) as everyone rejoiced together in the memory of our risen Saviour.

Celebrating Pentecost

The resurrected Christ told his followers to wait in Jerusalem for the coming of the Holy Spirit. They did and we are still celebrating the coming of the Spirit and the birth of the church.

In the book *A Continual Feast* the author describes the imaginative ways medieval Christians celebrated the feast of Pentecost. Apparently churches actually constructed "Holy Ghost" holes in the ceiling. As trumpets sounded a huge gold disc was lowered with a picture of a white dove painted on it and the feast began.[27] We don't plan to cut a hole in our roof but this year we are going to create an imaginative feast to celebrate the birth of the church.

Celebrating Kingdomtide

The final season of the church year is usually called "Ordinary Time", which we find less than exciting. Some call this season by a much more compelling title "Kingdomtide". . . a time to build the church birthed at Pentecost. One of the most powerful literary images of entering the kingdom is found in John Bunyan's *Pilgrim's Progress.* "Kingdomtide is about living in the Kingdom now so that we, like Christian, will be able to enter the true kingdom of which this is but a shadow."[28]

Both of us love to use the scriptures for this season to visualize how our lives, communities and the larger world would be transformed if God's kingdom broke into our world today. We visualize a world in which the City of Shalom replaces the Boom City Mall and justice finally comes to the poor and transformation to the nations. As you can imagine visualizing what the return of Christ will mean not only to our lives but God's world can lead to some very jubilant celebration.

Richard Foster states in his important book *Prayer: Finding the Heart's True Home*: "For too long we have been in a far country: a country of noise and hurry and crowds, a country of climb and push and shove, a country of frustration and fear and intimidation. And he (God) welcomes us home: home to serenity, and peace and joy, home to friendship and fellowship and openness, home to intimacy and acceptance and affirmation . . . The key to this home, this heart of God, is prayer."[29] Foster is right. Many of us find ourselves drowning in the noise of a far country. The invitation that comes to us in Jesus is to

Off Ramp No. 10

Creating a way of life you will love

On this off ramp we invite you to take your mission statement and your list of goals and actually begin the process of creating a new way of life by reinventing your timestyle and lifestyle.

1. In light of your mission statement and goals change your schedule and budget both to reduce the pressure on your life and to release more of your time and money to put first things first.

2. Now it is creativity time. Use some of the time and resources you have freed up to create new celebrations of your faith and new liturgies for your life.

3. Next, outline specific ways you will use some of the time and money you have freed up to actually implement your goals and your mission statement.

4. Finally, share with your community or Christian friends your proposed areas of change in your stewardship of your time and money and your new liturgy of life and ask them to hold you accountable. And do invite them to your new celebrations.

find our way home to the best that God has for us . . . a life that reflects the celebration, rhythm and compassion of God's new order. God invites us to discover the joy of faith not only as *doing* but as *being* as well. And whole-life faith that is both being and doing is only possible in community with other followers of Jesus. In the next chapter we will help you discover how to actually use your mission statement and some of the time you freed up to become more involved in the adventure of making a difference in your world.

Notes

1. Dorothy C. Bass, *Receiving the Day: Christian Practices for Opening the Gift of Time*, San Francisco: Jossey-Bass, p. 28.

2. Jon and Sylvia Ronsvalle, "The State of Church Giving through 1997", Champaign: Empty Tomb Inc., 1999, p. 46.
3. www.christian-research.org.uk/sam12.htm
4. Data from English Church Attendance Survey, quoted by Matt Bird, The Gen X Survey, Quadrant, July 2001 p. 1.
5. Jon and Sylvia Ronsvalle, "The State of Church Giving through 1998", Champaign: Empty Tomb Inc., 2000, p.7.
6. Ronsvalle, pp. 7 and 42.
7. Data from Family Expenditure Surveys quoted in CAF Research Dimensions 2000 Online, Briefing Paper 7, p. 1.
8. Craig L. Blomberg, *Neither Riches or Poverty: A Biblical Theology of Material Possessions*, Grand Rapids: Eerdmans, 1999, p. 136.
9. Jon and Sylvia Ronsvalle, "The State of Church Giving Through 1998", Champaign: Empty Tomb Inc., 2000, p. 7.
10. Jacques Ellul, *Money and Power*, Downers Grove: InterVarsity Press, 1984, p. 77.
11. Walter E. Pilgrim, *Good News to the Poor: Wealth and Poverty in Luke/Acts*, Minneapolis: Augsburg Fortress, 1981, p. 95.
12. Craig L. Blomberg, *Neither Riches or Poverty, A Biblical Theology of Material Possessions*, Grand Rapids: Eerdmans, 1999, p. 136.
13. Rod Sider, *Rich Christians in an Age of Hunger*, London: Hodder & Stoughton, 1978, p. 149.
14. R. Scott Rodin, *Stewards in the Kingdom: A Theology of Life in All Its Fullness*, Downers Grove: InterVarsity Press, 2000, pp. 42–43.
15. L. W. Cowie and John Selwyn Gummer, *The Christian Calendar*, Springfield: G.C. Merridian Company, 1974, p. 37.
16. Donald Kraybill, *The Upside Down Kingdom*, Scottsdale: Herald Press, 1990, p. 137.
17. Holly J. Lebowitz, "What is Right With This Picture?" *Sojourners*, January – February 2001, p. 36.
18. Francine Klagsbrun, *Jewish Days: A Book of Jewish Life*

and Culture, New York: Farrar Straus Giroux Publishers, 1996, pp. 11–13.

19. N. T. Wright, *The Challenge of Jesus*, Downers Grove: InterVarsity Press, 1999, pp. 44–45.

20. Esther de Waal, *The Celtic Way of Prayer: The Recovery of the Religious Imagination*, New York: Doubleday, 1997, p. 53.

21. Dorothy C. Bass, *Receiving the Day: Christian Practices for Opening the Gift of Time*, San Francisco: Jossey-Bass, 2000, p. 77.

22. Bass, p. 72.

23. Marva J. Dawn, *Keeping the Sabbath Wholly*, Grand Rapids: Eerdmans, 1989, p. 147.

24. Donna Fletcher Crow, *Seasons of Prayer: Rediscovering Classic Prayers Through the Christian Calendar*, Kansas City: Beacon Hill Press, 2000, p. 13.

25. Crow, p. 23.

26. Gertrud M. Nelson, *To Dance with God*, New York: Paulist Press, 1986, p. 139.

27. Evelyn Birge Vitz, *A Continual Feast*, San Francisco: Ignatius Press, 1985, p. 211.

28. Crow, p. 99.

29. Richard J. Foster, *Prayer: Finding the Heart's True Home*, San Francisco, HarperCollins: 1992, p. 1.

6

Seeking First the Kingdom in Community

THE RISING
Let us go forth,
In the goodness of our merciful father
In the gentleness of our brother Jesus
In the radiance of his Holy Spirit
In the faith of the apostles,
In the joyful praise of the angels,
In the holiness of the saints,
In the courage of the martyrs.
Let us go forth,
In the wisdom of our all-seeing Father
In the patience of our all-loving brother,
In the truth of the all-knowing Spirit,
In the learning of the apostles
In the gracious guidance of the angels,
In the patience of the saints,
In the self control of the martyrs,
Such is the path for all servants of Christ,
The path from death to eternal life.[1]

The infamous *Wittenberg Door* magazine dedicated an issue to
Christian community a few years ago. The front cover sported a
photo of eight "deeply religious" believers sitting in a circle with
their Bibles open . . . in a hot tub. It wasn't clear what the faithful
were wearing. As they had hoped, the magazine received a huge
response to their cover photo. But the fact is that sometimes
Christians do have a problem taking community seriously because
it really is counter to much of the deeply ingrained individualism
and autonomy of our Western culture. Ironically it is also counter
to a strongly reinforced individualism in many of our churches as
well. As we have seen, this high valuing of individualism which
comes at a very high cost to our lives, our spirituality and our relationships, is one of the cardinal values of Boom City.

Finding the focus

We can only be healthy human beings to the extent that we invest time in building significant relationships and connect to supportive communities. We can only be vital Christians to the extent that we are in communities where we are known, loved, nurtured and held accountable. In fact it is impossible to answer the biblical call to be radical whole-life disciples, stewards and servants on our own. To implement our mission statements and goals and to reinvent how we use time and money we must have the support, prayers and accountability of community. We can only faithfully follow Jesus Christ in community with other sisters and brothers who have made the same unequivocal commitment to seek first the kingdom.

We strongly believe that the first call of gospel isn't to proclamation, yet we are committed to evangelism. Nor do we believe the first call of the gospel is to social action, yet we are devoted to helping the poor. We believe the first call of the gospel of Christ is to *incarnation*. Only as we begin to flesh out in community with other sisters and brothers something of the right-side-up values of the kingdom do we have any basis to speak or to act. We need to create "communities of subversion" that enable believers to resist and subvert the seductions of Boom City. But we also need to create communities of worship, celebration and service that reflect a very different vision for the good life and better future. Lesslie Newbigin explains, "What did occupy the centre of Jesus' concern was the calling and binding to himself of a living community of men and women who would be the witnesses of what he was and did. The new reality that he introduced into history was to be continued through history in the form of a community, not in the form of a book."[2]

In this chapter we will define what incarnational community looks like by first re-examining our contemporary notions of what it means to be the church and to be in community. Then we will seek to find in scripture a new image of both church and community. Finally, we will share a range of models of community showing how other believers are seeking to flesh out something of the shalom future of God in imaginative new ways.

In search of community

Coming to terms with individualism

One morning Judith, a new missionary to a small village in Ghana, accompanied the women to the well – a walk of some two miles. As they walked they shared stories, laughed and sang and told jokes. The banter continued as they drew the water and the children who accompanied them were soon soaked as they splashed each other and played. On the way back to the village, Judith described the home she came from in the US and proudly told the women that in her country each home had its own water supply inside the house. She expected the women to be impressed with such convenience but to her surprise they weren't. "How lonely for you," they responded. "When do you talk to your neighbours?"

One of the most noticeable changes in Western culture over the last century has been the growing isolation of individuals. As we have seen there has also been growing emphasis on seeing ourselves as individual consumers whose primary task is to keep the economy booming. This may be great for the economy but it doesn't seem to be doing us much good as people. Particularly concerning is Robert Putnam's research in *Bowling Alone*. Putnam documents that more and more people in America are disconnecting from face-to-face relationships and all kinds of organizations including the church. Putnam blames this relational disconnect for the rapidly escalating levels of depression and suicide, particularly among younger generations. "Between 1950 and 1995 the suicide rate among adolescents aged fifteen to nineteen more than quadrupled, while rates among young adults aged twenty to twenty-four, beginning at a higher level, nearly tripled."[3] According to the World

Health Organization depression will be the most common illness in the world by 2020. The growing fragmentation of families and the breakdown of community connectedness is a major cause.[4]

Looking for community in all the wrong places

Psychologist Paul Wachtel reported that more and more of us seem to be seeking to meet our needs for intimacy and community through the things we buy, but it doesn't work.[5] The marketers of Boom City have actually created two new forms of community not to meet our needs for intimacy but to enable them to sell us more stuff. In the first model marketers actually keep detailed information on our individual tastes and preferences and so they can assign us to groups that have a similar profile. For example, if you are a part of the cluster they call "the pools and patio" these marketers know where you live and exactly how to manipulate your consumer choices.[6] David Lyon, in *Jesus in Disneyland,* informs us that it is "our consumer conduct" that "increasingly holds things together, culturally and socially."[7]

In the second group are people who actually join a community of consumption. "'Community' has become one of the hottest buzzwords in marketing" thanks to the internet which brings people together in affinity groups of all types. Harley Davidson pulled itself from the brink of extinction by forming Harley owner groups and getting them together to have community around their common passion. "To really experience the full value of a product community is the best way to do it . . . it can be a transforming experience."[8] Are you looking for a community where you can be bonded together in a "transforming" shared shopping experience or something more? More and more Christian families tell us that the primary activity that bonds them together isn't worship or service but consuming together. Their primary family bonding is around TV, trips to the shopping mall and Big Macs together. Where is your community bonding?

Off Ramp No. 11

Checking in ... what bonds your community together?

Deep down I am sure we all recognize we need community. But what kind of community?

1. Describe people you know who seem to live very individual lives largely disconnected from community and then describe the consequences it seems to have in their lives.

2. Describe any groups in your neighbourhood or church where conversation revolves primarily around things they consume from new clothes and cars to recreational vehicles and places to holiday.

3. To what extent is your bonding with family or friends around the things you consume together like TV, Big Macs or trips to the shops? How much of your conversation with friends at church or neighbours is about activities of consumption?

4. Now reflect back over your life and design a mental collage of your best memories of family or community. If you have time design a real collage of your memories either using snapshots from your community experience or with pictures cut out of magazines that capture the spirit of your community experience. Which if any of these memories were related to close family times or to your faith? Share your answers including your best memories of community with your small group or your friend and pray for new possibilities.

How we got community wrong

While churches do offer a place for people to come together and find vital community, too often we unwittingly sanction the values of Boom City rather than challenge them. In fact, evangelical historian George Marsden states that the history of American evangelicalism is a history of supporting the middle class values of American culture. He writes that there was no appeal to "abandon most of the standards of the respectable middle class way of life. It was to those standards that people were converted."[9] Mike Riddell, in *Threshold of the Future*, made the point in another way. Western Christians buy into "middle class aspirations such as consumerism, individualism, careerism, and security".[10] Are faith and culture supposed to be fused together?

We have not only sanctioned those values; tragically we have even allowed them at times to shape how we view the church. For example, far from challenging the growing individualism and consumerism of modern culture many churches have bought into it. Both large megachurches and smaller local congregations have settled for a view of the church that is little differentiated from a consumer mall. Briefly stated the church is reduced to a place I go once a week to have my individual "consumer" needs met. If the church can't meet my needs then I will "shop around" until I can find one that does. A growing number of megachurches in the US are drawing people away from smaller congregations that can't begin to match the range of consumer options they offer including weight rooms, saunas and food courts. Rodney Clapp writes that "Trained as consummate consumers, we learn to adopt even religious faith tentatively, with an eye to what may be around the next bend."[11]

For many our implicit theology of the church (ecclesiology) is that it is a building we go to once a week to have our individual needs met. And over the past two decades we have seen an increased focus on meeting the individual needs of people inside the building and a growing disinterest in the needs of those outside. Most churches we work with in North America don't sponsor any ministries in their own communities and seem to be becoming more self-involved.

South African missiologist David Bosch said that only after the Reformation did the church become a building you went to once a week. Before the Reformation it often was seen as a community you lived in seven days a week where you also happened to worship.[12] Not only is our notion of the church in trouble: believers in the US, Canada, the UK and Down Under tell us that they are having trouble finding vital community in the congregations they attend. Is your church a place you find vital community? We sincerely believe that our declining attendance and declining levels of involvement are caused in part by our seriously flawed notions of what it means to be the church. We have settled for models that often do more to promote individualism and the commodification of faith than to foster vital community and active outreach.

In search of biblical community

To find viable, enriching community we must begin by asking a very important question: what does it mean to be the church? Is it simply a place we go once a week to meet our individual needs? Or is the biblical notion of church and community somehow different from these culturally accommodated models of the church?

God's first family

In *Family at the Crossroads* Rodney Clapp argues that we have our notion of the church dead wrong. He argues that a biblical view of the church is not of going to a building once a week to have our individual needs met. He insisted Jesus taught that the new community he was forming was intended to be the "first family". Clapp makes a convincing case that the biological family is not God's primary institution on earth. The church is. In fact in one of the very few passages where Jesus mentions family, Jesus turned away his biological mother and brothers and declared instead, "Whoever does God's will is my brother and sister and mother" (Mark 3:31–35). "Jesus' primary family is not composed of those who share the same genetic makeup, but those who share his obedient spirit." Clapp adds, "Jesus creates a new family. It is the new first family, a family of his followers that now demands primary allegiance."[13] This new first family is a family with a mission. We are called both to flesh out something of God's new order and to advance the purposes of that new order in the world.

From the very beginning of this drama God's plan was to create a new people, a new community that reflected something of the character of God's new order. Abraham and Sarah became the first parents of this new family through which God's new order would transform the world. The children of Israel were called to be a living breathing model of the shalom of God in all areas of their shared life. As we know sometimes they got it right but often they became almost indistinguishable from the surrounding nations. But God never gave up on this project.

The coming of Christ gave this project a fresh start. One of the first things that Jesus did, at the beginning of his ministry, was to start a new community that was to be an incarnational expression of God's new order. This new community became a welcoming family to anyone who turned to God in repentance and faith. In its early days, it really functioned much more like a large extended family on the move than a programmatic institution you attended once a week to have your needs met. Look at this snapshot from Acts. "All the believers were together and had everything in common. Selling their possessions and goods, they gave to anyone as they had need. Every day they continued to meet together in the temple courts. They broke bread in their homes and ate together with glad and sincere hearts, praising God and enjoying the favor of all the people. And the Lord added to their number daily those who were being saved" (Acts 2:44–47).

British theologian Michael Green describes the incredible impact that new incarnational counter-cultural community had on the world around them. "They made the grace of God credible by a society of love and mutual care which astonished pagans and was recognized as something entirely new. It lent persuasiveness to the claim that the new age had dawned in Christ. The word was not only announced but seen in community by those who were giving it flesh. The message of the kingdom became more than an idea. A new human community had sprung up and looked very much like the new order to which the evangelist had pointed. Here love was given daily expression; reconciliation was actually occurring; people were no longer divided into Jews and Gentiles, slave and free, male and female. In this community the weak were protected, the stranger welcomed. People were healed, the poor found justice. Everything was shared. Joy abounded and ordinary lives were filled with praise."[14] It was through this very supportive new community that followers were able to become whole-life disciples living by very different values than those of the dominant culture.

Darrell Guder states that "This communal reality of holy living, mutual support and sacrificial service the New Testament calls *koinonia*. Challenging the old competitive order of independence, self-interest, and private privilege (*idios*) Christian community indicates a new collaborative order of interdependence, shared responsibility, mutual instruction and commonality (*koinos*). Within this new company of believers studying, sharing, eating and praying together, the promised fulfillment of creation is visible, tangible, and experienced, even though not yet perfected."[15] Clearly this new community became a compelling alternative to the dominant culture both for their time and ours. Guder emphasizes "The purpose of missional communities is to be a source of radical hope, to witness to the new identity and vision, the new way of life that has become a social reality in Jesus Christ through the power of the Holy Spirit. . . . As a sign, foretaste, agent and instrument of God's reconciling love and forgiveness, the church makes Jesus Christ visible in the world. . . . The forming of Christian community is therefore not an option but the very lifestyle and vocation of the church."[16]

Reinventing the church as God's first family

If we reinvented the church to be God's first family, what might it look like? Like the emerging youth churches it would probably be more relational and less institutional. It would be a place where we are known, loved and held accountable. Instead of simply reflecting the values of the Boom City culture it would both challenge them and become a new incarnational sample of God's kingdom. It would no longer be a place you go to have your individual needs met, but rather a place where you were being conformed to the image of Christ. Instead of focusing primarily on meeting the needs of people inside the building the church would become much more of a missional community finding creative ways to involve all members in extending God's love to the world. We want to share some snapshots of what that reinvented community of faith might look like. First, this new community needs to be centred on both worshipping the living God and learning to listen to our God.

A new community centred in worshipping God

Frankly, we have worshipped in a number of both traditional and contemporary services that lack any sense of serious vitality or engagement. We have much to learn about creative approaches to worship from the postmodern church that is experimenting with both traditional and non-traditional approaches aimed at engaging the outsider.

At the very centre of vital community life must be vital worship. It was in the worship of the God who had taken on a "human face" in Christ that many people of different races, cultures and economic strata were able to come together. One of the most creative books on alternative worship, *The Prodigal Project*, states: "Good worship connects the lives of the worshipers to the life of God."[17] Craig Dykstra shares another insight, "In worship we see and sense who it is that we are to be . . ."[18] John Drane writes "For the earliest Christians worship was not a withdrawal from the world like some of the mystery religions; the experience of worship opened them out to the needs and concerns of the world."[19] In other words, like Isaiah in the temple, one of the places we are likely to hear God call us beyond ourselves is in the place of worship.

For us the Eucharist is the centre of worship. Somehow in sharing in the mystery of the bread and wine we become

bonded not only to the Living God but also to a huge community which has gone before us, including our loved ones. In a
very real sense every time we sit down at table to share the bread
and the wine we are joining in a foretaste of the great homecoming banquet at the return of Christ in which all things will
be made new. The best that has ever been will be alive again!
"The Holy Communion is our supreme experience of all God's
people coming together, not on our terms but on God's terms.
It is our vision of unity being actualized . . . At the table and in
all our *shalom* we focus finally on him who is the embodiment
of *shalom*."[20]

Listening to God

Of course the first way we listen to God is in the preaching of
the word. What we suggest is for those who are called to preach
and teach the scripture not to restrict their focus exclusively to
our spiritual lives and relationships but to place much more
emphasis on how the word of God also challenges us to change
our cultural values. But God speaks to us not just through the
preached word but through community as well. Remember in
the Active Listening Process we gave you an opportunity to discover the value of taking time to listen for God's call.

At the start of a conference we led for Aboriginal Christian
leaders in a retreat centre outside Christine's hometown of
Sydney, Australia, the organizer, Ray Minnecon, did something
very unusual. He chose a group of seven older men and women
to listen for God's guidance during the weekend, to pray for us
and share what they believed God was saying. It was the first
time we had ever experienced anything like this. Periodically we
stopped for the elders to pray. We sat in silence until one or two
elders shared their sense of what God was saying. We not only
had a profound sense of God's presence but were also recipients
of something of the wisdom of God.

Many charismatic and evangelical groups encourage individual listening to God. Though we do believe God leads us as
individuals we feel corporate guidance is more reliable in part

because it is less likely to be influenced by self-interest. Quakers have taught for years about the enormous value of listening for God's guidance through community. They call this process "listening for clearness". Often, when a Quaker faces a major decision regarding relocating, changing jobs, getting married or moving into a full-time mission position, they call together a group of friends to listen corporately for God's guidance. Remarkably they even use the "listening for clearness" process in their business meetings.

Typically the meeting begins with a worship time in which people centre on God and God's direction. When the meeting hits a particularly troubling issue they stop the proceedings for a time of listening for clearness. After perhaps 20 minutes of silence a clerk is appointed to solicit input on the issue before them from individuals who feel led to speak. The clerk is expected to be very direct and ask questions like, "Do you believe this is a message truly from the Holy Spirit or is it coming from your own agenda?" Let's look at the emergence of some new models of community.

Exploring new forms of community for the 21st century

There is an array of interesting ways believers can follow Christ in community. We invite you to explore some of these models with us. This might help you find a vital faith community to support you in your journey into a whole-life faith. Keep your pad handy and write down any models that stir your spirit.

Rediscovering small groups

The thriving edge of the church in Britain is growing because of the re-emergence of a form of small group called cell groups. Essentially cell groups provide places where believers are known and nurtured in the faith. When a cell becomes too large it divides into two cells which grow until they divide again.

Small groups and cell groups are also common in North America and Down Under. They provide an opportunity even for established churches to move beyond the institutional and programmatic to create a serious expression of genuine family life with both support and accountability for its members. More and more people become part of small groups at work, at leisure or even on-line. However we are not convinced that it is possible to have real community in other than face-to-face relationships.

We came across one unique form of small group in Melbourne, Australia. Sharon, a mother with two small children, invited three of her friends, who are also homemakers, to share five mornings a week together. They gather at a different house each morning, and while one person looks after the kids the others tackle the housework – Sharon told us it goes much faster when they work together rather than alone. When the housework is done, they pray together, read the Bible or share concerns. On other mornings they just share fun and fellowship. One morning a week they also do chores for a disabled friend who is unable to do her own housework.

To implement your new mission statement and goals and to reinvent your timestyle and lifestyle you will need the support and accountability of a community. Therefore, we strongly recommend you join or start a small support group for the journey forward and ask them to hold you accountable for your goals. A church in Indiana created a unique approach to accountability that tends to make many Christians with their autonomous approach to faith a little uncomfortable when we share it. Everyone in the church is part of small groups where they study scripture and pray for one another. Twice a year each person is invited to bring their time schedule and financial budget to openly share with the group, asking how they can steward their lives to put God's purposes first. We are a part of a small group with five friends who share our passion for the kingdom. They have no reluctance in holding us accountable for our life, faith and ministry.

The postmodern church

Over the past ten years a young people's church movement has emerged in Britain, Australia, New Zealand, Canada and the United States that is much more relational than most established churches. There are nearly 1,000 new church plants in the US started by 20- and 30-year-olds. These youth churches have no bureaucracies, no committees and virtually no formal programmes. Typically they have just enough structure to keep things together. In fact they frequently have serious disdain for some of the "boomer church" models that seek to replicate their church programmes all over the world. These postmodern churches emphasize the need for each new plant to create offerings that uniquely fit its own context and tend to be strongly missional. We believe one of the major reasons these churches are enjoying rapid growth is because they have created more relational models of church that engage a disconnected generation. One of the most helpful books on the emerging church and postmodern culture is *Get a Grip on the Future Without Losing Your Hold on the Past* by Gerard Kelly.[21]

Solomon's Porch is a growing new church plant of some 200 members in the Twin Cities (Minneapolis/St Paul). It is an example of this new, more relational younger expression of church. As pastor Doug Pagitt described this experiment in church planting to me he was very enthused by what God was doing in their midst. The congregation is very outwardly focused in mission working with single parent mothers in their neighbourhood and is planning to buy a house to serve these women and their kids. Doug and 50 of his friends are planning a trip to Guatemala to partner with churches there to build houses with the poor.

Community is the defining term for this new plant but as Doug explained it is a very free-form, organic community. There are community meals Wednesday night, after worship Sunday night and spontaneously during the week. During these gatherings natural relationships form and people become family to one another. Doug stressed that there are no programmes, no curriculums, not even small groups. He emphasized that whenever they come together they see themselves connecting to both the historic church and the global church. The focus in these gatherings is not on individual need-meeting but on growing community and making a difference in the world. At the centre of their life together is worship and at the centre of worship is the Eucharist. Doug describes it like a house party in which he and his wife Shelley, their two biological kids and their two adopted kids welcome everyone to the table for the banquet feast.

These new youth churches work instinctively like the early Celtic Christian communities of the 6th and 7th centuries. Instead of trying to get people to consider the claims of the gospel, make a decision and then welcome them into community, they start the other way round. They welcome individuals into community first complete with all the warts, wrinkles and addictions. The Christians simply build relationships and love these folks as they try to pay attention to what the Holy Spirit is doing in their lives. As these people are drawn to the gospel incarnated in the lives of the young believers they are also drawn into a journey that frequently leads to vital faith. In *The Celtic Way of Evangelism* George Hunter describes why this approach spread the gospel like wildfire not only in Ireland, Scotland and England but also throughout Europe, while the Roman church experienced very little success in evangelism. He writes, "Evangelism is now about 'helping people to belong so that they can believe.'"[22]

Mars Hill Fellowship is a rapidly growing church plant in Seattle with over 650 mainly 20- and 30-year-olds. The Celtic Christian approach to evangelism of belonging before believing works very effectively for them. Like Solomon's Porch they invite people into all kinds of informal relationships around food, video parties and celebrations. But they also sponsor two houses, one for single women called Noon Day and one for single men called White Horse Inn.

Jennifer, who is one of the leaders in Noon Day, related how they welcomed a young woman named Tracy into their house fully aware that she wasn't a believer. Jennifer and the other Christian women accepted Tracy warmly into their community. After a few weeks she expressed interest in taking communion. Jennifer asked "Do you understand that taking communion represents committing your life to God?" Tracy responded positively and now she is one of the Christian leaders of the house.

A group of young Christians in the UK connected with a movement called the World Wide Message Tribe found another way to give expression to the Celtic community approach to sharing their faith. A dozen of them moved into several apartments in a rundown housing estate called Eden in Manchester, England. They seek to be the shalom of God in that place and so have deliberately limited their work time to 20 hours a week to leave plenty of time to get to know their neighbours, play with the kids and share bangers and chips with their new friends.

Burnt Street House is part of the Blackburn Community Network in Melbourne, Australia. The five young people who live in this double apartment have a single mission – to become part of the larger community of Cambodian refugees who comprise most of their neighbours. They serve as tutors in the local primary school, volunteer in the community and actively lobby the government for social justice alongside their Cambodian neighbours.

Discovering the counter-cultural possibilities of community

One of the most intriguing aspects of this younger postmodern church is that it often questions the values of the dominant culture that the established church simply sanctions. For instance, a youth church of some 300 members in England called Warehouse decided to have a "Logo Fast Night". No one was allowed into worship on this particular night with a corporate brand anywhere on their bodies. More than that they had to bring some of their most expensive branded clothing with them to church to give away to help the poor.

We find many postmodern young people believe it is important to bring issues of transformation of culture right into worship. Steve Taylor, a very innovative 27-year-old Baptist minister in Auckland, New Zealand, planted a church for "postmodern pilgrims" called Graceway. He and his team developed some very creative rituals to help change the values that these young people grapple with on a daily basis. On one occasion they held an evening worship service entitled "What is your obsession?" The community gathered around café tables for dinner. Behind them an entire wall displayed "worship wallpaper". It was covered in advertisements from Nike, Calvin Klein and the Body Shop.

The worship service began with songs reminding the congregation of the beauty of God's creation. Then Steve led a discussion about the beauty, design and goodness of God's creation reflected in modern fashion. They talked about the richness of fabrics and textures. Then they confessed the obsessions with style and body image that held a number of them, particularly young women, in bondage. They concluded by putting on their own fashion show, dressing up in clothes from the local second hand shop. They had fun laughing at themselves and some of the absurd fashions that they created. Steve offered a 10-minute reflection on committing our entire lives to Jesus Christ and inviting him and his kingdom to become the obsession of our lives instead of the style, image and status of the modern culture to which we have become addicted.

Recovering the possibility of religious orders

Religious orders are the oldest form of Christian community. Trappist, Franciscan and Benedictine orders still girdle the globe. But they are in rapid decline in most Western countries. Female and Male religious orders in America have declined 50 per cent from 1965 to 2000. Today there are only 79,814 sisters and 5,662 brothers left. Leaders of the religious orders are mounting an imaginative campaign to entice young people into considering religious vocations. They invite them to a three-day monastic retreat to check out this option.[23] Many young people are looking more to lay monastic options instead of a lifetime commitment to a religious order.

When we travel we visit all kinds of Christian communities to try to gain a sense of what God is doing. You can read about alternative European communities in Jeanne Hinton's book *Communities: The stories and spirituality of twelve European communities.*[24] And *Living Differently* published by the Uniting Church of Australia describes 20 experimental communities in Australia.[25]

There are a number of communities in North America that are worth a visit too – from Jesus People USA in Chicago to Jubilee Partners in Georgia. Jon Trott, editor of Jesus People's Cornerstone Magazine lives in a small apartment with his family. When I asked if it felt like a sacrifice to live this kind of modest community lifestyle his response was immediate. "Not at all," Jon said. "Life is a trade-off . . . no one gets all they want. But I wouldn't trade my way of life, which is rich in community relations for the biggest house in the suburbs with a fleet of new cars! I am convinced I am way ahead of those folks." If you would like to learn more about some of the alternative communities in North America get a copy of *Fire, Salt, and Peace: Intentional Communities Alive in North America.*[26] You will find a number of the communities listed offer hospitality to those who want to see first hand what life in these residential communities is like.

Discovering the possibilities of co-operative community

For all kinds of reasons we really believe we need to examine our unquestioned and unexamined commitment to the single family detached housing model. First, this model is not inherently sacred. In fact if we actually designed housing to reflect the more co-operative communities normative in the book of Acts we would never wind up with an individual single family detached model where we don't talk to the neighbours on either side. Second, it is a very expensive model. Most Americans spend between a third of a million dollars and 3 million dollars over 30 years for this model. As we have seen many young people are spending over 50 per cent of their income on rent and mortgage. This is money or time not invested in the work of God's kingdom. Third, we believe that the nuclear family doesn't have any possibility of standing up to the relentless pressures to conform to the expectations of Boom City.

If we are deadly serious about being whole-life disciples and incarnational communities we need to reinvent not only our housing and churches. Alvin Toffler in his classic, *Future Shock*, says that we also need to create "enclaves of the future".[27] Instead of settling for church as a place to go once a week and single family detached houses we spend a huge amount of our life energy and income paying for, how about people of faith creating a broad range of new "enclaves of the future" that more authentically reflect the values of the City of Shalom instead of the obsessions of Boom City? We suggest we create a spectrum of both new forms of co-operative housing and new residential church plants where we live in community with the people we worship. Not to pull out of the world, but to engage the world.

I suggest we begin this journey by learning from the co-operative housing communities started in Denmark 25 years ago. Fear not! These are not the hippie dippy communes of the sixties. They are more like a condo with a purpose. Imagine 75 people living in a condo, all with their own units. Instead of backyard and front yard . . . they have one place where all the kids play together and another where everyone gardens together. There is typically a common dining room, where like an extended family, everyone eats together once or twice a week. Singles, widows and families with kids report they love this model because they have closer relationship with their neighbours.

Currently there are 50 co-housing communities in America and another 150 on the drawing board. Most are being built by social progressives who want to create intentional communities in which to raise their kids that reflect the values of environmental care. Wouldn't it be great if Christians took our kingdom values this seriously? Some are. A small group of Christians in Oakland, California, took their biblical values so seriously they invented one new model of a kingdom community.

Creating a Christian co-op in Oakland

Rockridge United Methodist Church is one of those unusual churches with mainly young members. Rockridge is located in an inner-city area in Oakland, California and wants to provide a serious witness for the kingdom in the neighbourhood. This congregation is more interested in qualitative than quantitative growth. Like Church of the Savior in Washington DC they raised the bar by expecting every disciple to spend at least half an hour a day in scripture and prayer. Everyone is expected to start giving 10 per cent of their income to the work of God and then as God prospers them to ratchet it up from there. Every member participates not only in weekly worship but in small mission groups that use some of the rigours of Wesleyan class meetings to hold one another accountable for their spiritual and stewardship disciplines. Each small missions group is involved one other evening a week in some form of witness or service. What if your churches raised the bar and put more emphasis on qualitative instead of quantitative growth? We would probably have fewer disciples but they would certainly be much more invested in a radical whole-life faith that would have a much greater impact in their communities.

In 1996 one of these small mission groups at Rockridge Methodist sensed God was calling them to build a co-operative housing project in the community where they go to church. The design and construction took a while but recently they moved in. When we visited the Temescal Community we saw a series of bright, pastel-coloured, two-storey homes clustered around a mini-soccer field for the kids. A small ancient barn has been given over to the teenagers and there is a common dining room and kitchen that can accommodate 40. The community usually eats together twice a week but the dining room also serves as a community and neighbourhood meeting place. Altogether there are nine units, seven of which are new construction. One of the units is designed for families in transition. They all have solar collectors on their roofs, which provides 85 per cent of their electricity. Very good news in California these days! A thousand square foot organic garden provides vegetables and fruit for the entire community.

Christian education isn't an hour on Sunday. The adults all nurture the kids through learning experiences all week long, including helping them decode the messages from Boom City. Instead of private educational options parents send their kids to the neighbourhood Emerson Elementary. They also send volunteers from their church to the school to redeem it for all the kids in the neighbourhood. They share God's shalom through block parties and art festivals for the entire Temescal neighbourhood. Tom Prince told us that prior to entering this community he felt "the circles of my life were pulling me apart." Now he lives with his family in the same neighbourhood where they go to church and he teaches. Their vision statement reads, "We live in God's creation. We love God, each other, our neighbours and care for God's creation."[28] Thank God for their creative faith.

Creating Christian co-op housing everywhere

We are brainstorming with David Vandervort, an architect friend, about creating a co-housing community in Seattle. We would like to design the first project for young couples interested in involvement in urban ministry and then set up an interest-free revolving mortgage fund. If these couples will commit five years of their lives to urban mission they are granted a no-interest mortgage. Then they can pay off their mortgage in seven to ten years instead of a major share of their income going to a mortgage company for 30 years. Think about the possibilities in terms of whole-life stewardship. Not only could

Off Ramp No. 12
Finding our way home to community

There is no way you can continue this journey towards a purpose-driven life on your own. You can only do it in communities in which you are known, loved and held accountable.

1. It is time to hit the road again. Find what forms of community exist in your region from a vital small group programme in a local church, to a residential community, or even a co-housing project and get some friends to go visit with you, listening for God's guidance.

2. Share what you learned with your group or a friend and pray for guidance.

3. Pray over the list of community models we have shared or you have visited and ask God to guide you in ways to help the community you are already a part of to sharpen its focus or perhaps start a new expression of community.

4. Decide how God is calling you into community with other sisters and brothers and share that decision with your small study group or a friend. Ask them to hold you accountable to get started and find the support for all the progress you have made in this book in putting first things first.

much more of their life resources be invested to advance God's kingdom but they could become one of those living breathing incarnational examples of God's new order that people are so hungry to see.

As Australian theologian Athol Gill says in *Life of the Road,* "There is no such thing as a solitary Christian, an isolated disciple in the Gospels. To respond to the call of Jesus is to embark on a journey with others. There is no shortage of friends for the journey when you travel with Jesus."[29] The only way we can find God's best is to journey with others who have committed not only to seek first God's kingdom but also to give it flesh and blood in communities of celebration, subversion and service. It is new beginnings' time for those who have chosen to *live their lives on purpose.*

Internet resources

www.joshgen.org Matt Bird and the Joshua Generation team work with churches and organizations in the UK and around the world to help them invest in the new generation
www.youngleaders.org – Terra Nova project provides a forum for young leaders that deals with leadership, theology, the arts, compassion and justice
www.cohousing.org The co-housing network provides information and resources and links about co-housing projects around the world

Notes

1. Robert Van de Weyer, *Celtic Fire*, New York: Doubleday, 1991, p. 143.
2. Lesslie Newbigin, *The Open Secret*, Grand Rapids: Eerdmans, 1995, p. 52.
3. Robert D. Putnam, *Bowling Alone: The Collapse and Renewal of American Community,* New York: Simon & Schuster, 2000, pp. 260–261.
4. World Health Organization Report, 1997, p. 59.
5. Paul L. Wachtel, *The Poverty of Affluence: A Psychological Portrait of the American Way of Life*, New York: Free Press, 1985, pp. 61–65.
6. Michael J. Weiss, "The Beautiful and the Dammed: You are what you buy – wherever you live", *Utne Reader*, March/April 2000, p. 54.
7. David Lyon, *Jesus in Disneyland: Religion in Postmodern Times*, Cambridge: Polity Press, 2000, p. 79.
8. Kendra Nordin, "When products get a social life", *The Christian Science Monitor*, February 26, 2001, p. 16.

9. George Marsden, *Fundamentalism and American Culture*, Oxford: Oxford University Press, 1980, p. 38.

10. Mike Riddell, *Threshold of the Future: Reforming the Church in the Post-Christian West*, London: SPCK, 1998, p. 59.

11. Rodney Clapp, *Family at the Crossroads*, Downers Grove: InterVarsity Press, 1993, p. 64.

12. George Hunter, "Missional Vocation: Called and Sent to Represent the Reign of God", in *Missional Church: A Vision For the Sending Church in North America*, ed. Darrell L. Guder, Grand Rapids: Eerdmans, 1998, pp. 77–81.

13. Clapp, pp. 67–88.

14. Quoted in Jim Wallis, *The Call to Conversion: Recovering the Gospel For These Times*, San Francisco: Harper & Row, 1981, p. 15.

15. *Missional Church*, ed. Darrel L. Guder, p. 146.

16. Guder, p. 153.

17. Cathy Kilpatrick, Mark Pierson and Mike Riddell, *The Prodigal Project*, London: SPCK, 2000, p. 77.

18. Craig R. Dykstra, *Vision and Character*, New York: Paulist Press, 1981, p. 106.

19. John Drane, *Evangelism for a New Age: Creating Churches for the Next Century*, London: Marshall Pickering, 1994, p. 128.

20. Walter Brueggemann, *Living Toward a Vision: Biblical Reflections on Shalom*, New York: United Church Press, 1976, p. 51.

21. Gerard Kelly, *Get a Grip on the Future Without Losing Your Hold on the Past*, London: Monarch Books, 1999.

22. George G. Hunter III, *The Celtic Way of Evangelism: How Christianity Can Reach the West Again*, Nashville: Abingdon Press, 2000, p. 55.

23. Gustav Niebuhr, "Recruiting Pitch: Monastic Life for 3 Days", *New York Times*, January 13, 2001, p. 1 & A10.

24. Jeanne Hinton, *Communities: The stories and spirituality of*

twelve European communities, Guildford, Surrey: Eagle Publishing, 1993.

25. "Living Differently", A publication of the Christian Community Project, Uniting Youth Ministries, Commission on Missions, Synod of Victoria, Uniting Church In Australia, March 1999, Email, uym@kew.vic.uca.org.au.

26. David Janzen, *Fire, Salt and Peace: Intentional Communities Alive in North America*, Evanston, Ill: Shalom Mission Communities, A Division of Reba Place, 1996. Tel: 001–847–475–8715.

27. Alvin Toffler, *Future Shock*, New York: Random House, 1970, p. 349.

28. Tom Sine, "Not Your Father's Commune", *Regeneration Quarterly*, Spring 2000 edition, pp. 20–22.

29. Athol Gill, *Life of the Road*, Sydney: Anzea Publishers, 1989, p. 119.

7 Seeking First the Vocation of the Kingdom

Lord make me an instrument of your peace;
where there is hatred let me sow love,
where there is injury pardon, where there is doubt, faith;
where there is despair, hope; and where there is sadness, joy.
Divine Master, grant that I may not seek so much to be consoled as to
console,
to be understood as to understand, to be loved as to love;
For it is in giving that we receive, it is in pardoning that we are
pardoned,
and it is in dying that we are born to new life.

St Francis of Assisi

On a mission for God!

The beach front in Darwin, Australia swarmed with thousands of people enjoying themselves on a warm Saturday afternoon. Wonderful aromas of Brazilian, Indonesian and Aussie food wafted toward us as we followed the crowd to the centre of the promenade where the Australian Naval Band was playing some very hot blues music. To our astonishment two guys in black suits, black hats and shades were dancing, singing, and doing gymnastics to the music. We were watching an Aussie musical re-enactment of the vintage film *Blues Brothers*. The audience loved it. Apparently it had become something of a cult film in Australia, connecting to something deep within the Australian maverick psyche. It has played continuously in theatres Down Under since its original release.

Incredibly, when the sequel, *Blues Brothers 2*, was being filmed a couple years ago, 100 Australians sold their cars and quit their jobs, bought black suits, hats and shades and showed up unannounced for the first day of shooting in southern California. The producer was astonished. He explained they really didn't need 100 extra Blues Brothers but he was so impressed by their initiative and sacrifice that he put them all to work as extras.

Remember the story? Jake's brother picks him up from prison and they visit the Catholic school where they were troublemakers as kids. The head sister informs them that the school is being forced to close because of a $5,000 debt they can't pay. A short time later the Blues Brothers attend a very exuberant worship service in a black church where a bright light from heaven hits Jake and he has an epiphany. He cartwheels down the aisle and announces he "is on a mission for God!" He becomes absolutely single-minded in his mission to get their old band together to raise $5,000 and save the school from closure. And of course they do get the band back together, hold a packed out concert and raise the money. The saga ends in a wild chase scene through the streets of Chicago as the Blues Brothers do indeed deliver the $5,000 and save the day and the school.

The point is that even in producing the original comedy the producers recognized what it meant to be on a mission for God . . . to be single-minded in a cause that calls you beyond yourself. And one can't help but be impressed by the single-minded sacrifice of those 100 guys from Australia.

Those of us who claim to be followers of Christ need to recognize that faith isn't just about showing up at church and keeping things rolling. The call to follow Christ is a call for every believer to commit single-mindedly to a mission that calls us beyond ourselves. No kidding.

Finding the focus

To this point in the book we have mainly focused inwardly on our lives . . . how to find a focus and a liturgy of life that flows from our faith instead of modern culture. In Chapter five we tried to enable you to find a more celebrative way of life in which your faith determines both the rhythm and the priorities of your life instead of Boom City. If you were able to free up even a small amount of time in your week we want to show you how, by investing that time in making a difference, you will find a way of life that is not only less stressed and more festive, but a way of life that counts.

In this chapter we will help you actually put wheels under your mission statement and your goals related to mission, and field test them. We want you to find God's best . . . to experience the singular satisfaction of God using your mustard seed to have a real impact in the lives of others. We want to help you find what God is doing and find a creative way to join it. In other words we want to enable you to identify specific ways God can use your life either through your work hours or your discretionary time to advance God's purposes. For those who are already actively involved in some form of ministry, this chapter will hopefully help you sharpen your focus and perhaps provide some creative new ways to give expression to your call.

Finding that life focus isn't easy for any of us. Charlie Brown, of *Peanuts* fame, was shooting arrows into the wall of a garage. After each shot he took out a marker and drew a circle around the arrow so it was exactly in the centre. Lucy watched with interest. Finally she interrupted and said, "That's not the way it's done. You are supposed to draw the circle first and then see if you can shoot the arrow into the centre." Charlie immediately responded, "No thanks. In my system I never miss!"

We run into many Christians of all ages who, like Charlie Brown, draw a circle around where they land, and assume they are right on target. They assume that whatever they are doing with their lives is automatically what God intended. For example, Tom bumped into Janet, one of his former students, who had graduated from Seattle Pacific University six months earlier. Tom remembered that Janet had a very strong call to work in urban ministry. But when he asked what she was doing she responded, "I sell clothes at Nordstroms. It was the only job I could find so it must be God's will for my life." Doesn't Janet's response sound a little like shooting the arrow first and then drawing the circle around it? Do you know of people who assume whatever they are doing must somehow automatically be what God intended?

Looking back on a life with a difference

When you look back on your life, what legacy do you want to leave behind? Do you want to leave a legacy of your garage, attic and storage lockers filled with all the stuff you accumulated in one lifetime, plus lots of money in savings? Do you want to leave behind a wall full of plaques and accolades commemorating accomplishments in your work, profession or in sports? Or do you want to be able to look back and know God used your life to make a little difference in the world? One poll indicated that one of the major concerns for retirees is being able to look back and feel their lives counted for something.

Christine has never fully recovered from her work in the refugee camps in Thailand in the 1980s when she literally had children dying in her arms. Tom has never forgotten his first trip to Haiti in 1977 when he witnessed the grinding poverty that families contend with. Have you seen first hand some of the incredible poverty that many families beyond our borders or within our cities or rural areas have to contend with? Don't you struggle, as so many of us do, with coming back to our own very affluent situations trying to reconcile the disparity? Don't you feel motivated, even temporarily, to do something about it?

As we look at the world we see tremendous areas of spiritual and physical need on the one hand. On the other hand we see the church in the West endowed to overflowing with both financial resources and incredible time and talent. But as we saw, the Western church, including the church in Britain, seems to be haemorrhaging at many levels of involvement, from church attendance and giving patterns to lay involvement in things of faith. More and more people not only don't have daily time for prayer and scripture study, they don't have any time for witness or service during the week either. In the early eighties it was not unusual to find congregations in the US with more than 20 per cent of their members involved in witness or service outside home and church. Now our informal sampling suggests involvement in ministry has declined by at least 5 per cent to 15 per cent. In the UK congregations tend to be more involved in community service activities, but again our informal sampling suggests that Christians have become less involved as their lives get busier.

As mentioned earlier Christine looks back on her years of mission on the *Anastasis* as some of the happiest of her life, in spite of her chronic seasickness, because she discovered how God could use her life to make a difference for thousands of people who would not otherwise have access to either healthcare or to hope. For example, Linda was born with a cleft lip in a village in Togo. She should have been put to death because her deformity was viewed as a curse but her grandparents rescued her and took her to Lome, the capital city. Linda was 22 when the ship came to Lome. Her cleft lip was repaired. Not only her appearance was transformed but her whole life too. After the surgery Linda was reconciled to her parents and her village. She was able to tell everyone about a God who cared for her so much that people came from around the world to give her back her life.

Tom remembers the satisfaction of returning to a rural community in Haiti where he had supervised a community development project for World Concern. In this project a team helped valley leaders improve their agricultural production, start a rural health service and construct a road out of the land-locked valley. When he returned three years after the completion of the project he received a warm welcome from his friends. He was gratified to see all the programmes were still operating. In fact the valley leaders had actually pooled their resources to buy a truck. They took their own coffee beans to market, which increased their profits 250 per cent. Doctor Luke, one of the valley leaders, said that as a result of the increased income there had been a dramatic increase in the number of families with enough money to send their kids to primary school.

As you think back over your own life consider some of your most gratifying moments of discovering how God could use you to make a difference in the lives of others. Do you remember the sense of keen satisfaction you had? Are you involved in some form of ministry now? What is the best part of that involvement? If you are not currently involved in ministry, after this next off ramp, we will invite you to look at both our needy world and your mission statement to explore some new possibilities.

Seeking God's best

Deep down I believe we know what is God's best for our lives. It is being able to look back and realize God has used our mustard seed to make a little difference in the world. Jesus had it right. "Only as the corn of wheat falls into the ground and dies" is there any possibility of really finding the abundant life that God has for us. It is in losing that we find. The journey to the abundant life on which Jesus calls us begins by taking a good hard look at the world in which God has placed us.

Welcome to our world!

"Make the world your hobby" is the helpful advice of Paul Borthwick, a leading missions pastor committed to persuading every Christian to become a "world Christian". He and his wife make learning about God's world a high priority. They constantly read international news and the travel sections of the paper and watch films like *Out of Africa* and *A Passage to India*. There are world maps all over their house and a friend who caught the fever even has a shower curtain with a huge

Off Ramp No. 13
Checking out new possibilities

Let's take this off ramp to recall the satisfaction of opportunities to make a difference.

1. Using a tape recorder or your journal record some of those times you remember when God used your life to make a difference in the lives of others. Review those experiences each night before you go to bed, thanking God for those opportunities.

2. Take out your mission statement, read it over and start researching on the web or through your church or library different Christian and secular organizations that are already ministering in your areas of interest . . . learn as much as possible about them and their ministries.

3. Invite some of your friends to go with you to visit some of the ministries in your community that are making a difference for God's kingdom and learn as much as you can . . . regardless of whether these ministries relate directly to your areas of interest or not.

4. Ask the Holy Spirit to show you ways God might want you to re-focus your existing ministry, explore working with one of the groups you researched or possibly start a new ministry. Share all you have learned and what God is stirring within you regarding your involvement in ministry with your small group or with a friend.

map of the world embossed on it so his family can become world Christians as they shower.[1]

Let's take a quick look at the world that God loves and Christ died for. Let's look at the "fields white unto harvest" and examine some of the challenges of the next ten years for the world in which God has placed us as your first step to more clearly discern God's call on your life.

Selling Marie into slavery

The Saint Germaine family live in a small two-room hut with dirt-floors in the village of La Cayes, Haiti. Julia Saint

Germaine is cooking rice and yams together in a pot over an open fire in their yard. It is the only meal each day for her husband and six children. But as she stirs the pot Julia is very depressed because she realizes it won't be enough food. Her husband Jacques earns only $1.50 for a 12-hour day in road construction. Even though Julia sells a few mangos the total income is simply not enough to provide the essentials for their family. Julia realizes that she needs to talk to Jacques about selling another one of their children into bonded servitude.

Julia has never recovered from selling her seven-year-old daughter Marie into servitude three years ago. They lost all contact because Marie works for a family over 50 miles away. But Julia knows what Marie's life is like because she grew up as a "servant child" too. It means getting up at 5:30 to fix breakfast for the host family, working until 10 at night cleaning, carrying water and wood and getting only scraps to eat. The host family's biological kids go to school, celebrate birthdays and enjoy Christmas but Marie never gets a day off for any of these activities until she is liberated on her 18th birthday.

Thousands of families in Haiti and many other countries, particularly in Africa, struggle with the constant crisis of not having enough income to provide their children with even the basic essentials of life. In his album "Peace on Earth" Bono of U2 fame sings "I'm sick of all this/ Hanging around/ Sick of sorrow/ Sick of pain/ Sick of hearing again and again/ That there's gonna be/ Peace on Earth."[2] It isn't difficult to be overwhelmed by the enormity of the suffering that fills our world. Let me give you some of the statistics behind the lives of real people.

Listen to how the *World Christian Encyclopedia* describes the lives of the Saint Germaines and their neighbours around the world. 2.2 billion of the global poor don't have access to safe water. 700,000 live in shanty towns. 2 billion live in absolute poverty and earn under $2/day. 120 million are street children. 30 million kids die annually from hunger. Incredibly,

13 per cent of those living in absolute poverty or 250,000,000 people are our sisters and brothers in Jesus Christ. Isn't there something terribly wrong with our international Christian family when some of us are living palatially and other Christians can't even keep their kids fed?[3]

The hope was that the new global Boom economy would close the gap between our poorest and richest neighbours. The reality is that in this new assets-based economy the top 20 per cent have increased their share of global income while the bottom 20 per cent have actually lost their share. To make matters worse the UN World Employment Report 2001 is setting off alarm bells all over the world. It predicts that the global marketplace will need to create 500 million jobs by 2011 to absorb the huge number of young people from poor countries joining the workforce.[4] The church must do much more to help our poorest neighbours, by helping them start small businesses, credit unions, vocational education and job creation to secure the assets needed to play in this new global economy. Perhaps you feel God nudging you to work with an organization like Tearfund, which helps provide small loans to help the poor help themselves, or perhaps you are considering actually going abroad to be involved in mission.

Making ends meet with Stacey

Stacey Jackson gave Carol Johnson a huge tearful hug as the judge read his ruling in the Chicago municipal court. It all started when Stacey, age 29, was arrested for possession of crack cocaine. At the time she was pregnant and also had a 12-year-old daughter and a 9-year-old son. The court ordered her into drug treatment at Leland and her children were placed in foster care with their grandmother. That is where Stacey first met Carol, a volunteer to Leland House from Jesus People USA. Carol became a friend and saw her through a lot of ups and downs.

Stacey maintained a drug-free life for three years, completed a course in parenting and another in basic computer training.

During this rehab time Stacey also recommitted her life to Jesus Christ. At one point Stacey confided to Carol: "Without the Lord in my heart I know I wouldn't be alive today!" Stacey's church has begun to take an active role in helping her get her life back together.

So when the judge ruled that Stacey Jackson had completed all the conditions and returned her children to her custody there was a lot of hugging and celebrating. Stacey got a job working at a burger franchise at an entry level income of under $7 an hour. But like a lot of single mothers coming off welfare she is at an absolute loss as to how she can make that income stretch to cover basic living costs. The least expensive rental she can find for herself and her three kids is a two-bedroom apartment right on the edge of a high crime and drug area for $900 a month.[5]

Stacey is only one of thousands of mothers who are getting off welfare but not moving out of poverty. Many of them don't make enough to buy food, rent and child care too. In spite of this boom economy there has been a dramatic increase in homeless families and singles in the past 20 years in Britain and America and the situation is likely to get worse. According to a report by the London School of Economics, a third of British children – more than four million young people – are living in poverty; three times as many as in the 1970s.[6] Britain's largest homeless charity, Shelter, estimates that over 100,000 affordable homes will be required each year between 2001 and 2011 in order to meet the current need, but in 2000 only 17,000 units were completed.[7] In addition there is a rapidly increasing "digital divide" between the young from poor and privileged backgrounds, which will affect their employability. This means the church needs to do much more in providing computer education classes as well as inexpensive quality child care for mothers going back to school or going back to work. Do these growing areas of need stir you to make a difference in your community?

We all live in communities where growing numbers of our

young people, like Stacey, are at risk from alcohol and drug abuse. Anyone who has had first-hand experience with friends or family members caught up in such abuse knows how demonic and destructive addiction can be. Reportedly 14 million Americans are addicted to alcohol and another 14 million to drugs. Bingeing on alcohol is highest among young people in midwestern states like North Dakota. There is growing use of ecstasy among the young people in the East Coast rave scene. And heroin use is up among teens in many of our cities from San Francisco to Newark.[8] Do you sense God is calling you to reach out to the at-risk young in your community?

Going backwards in world evangelization

There is a tremendous hunger for spirituality in the UK, North America, and Down Under . . . particularly among the post-modern young, which is a tremendous opportunity for the church. The only problem is that what the established church is offering isn't very appealing to the unchurched young. Peter Brierley, at Christian Research in the UK, has some other bad news in terms of global mission. Today 28 per cent of the world's people identify themselves as some brand of Christian: Protestant, Catholic or Orthodox. But since global population is growing more rapidly than the church it will decline to 27 per cent and continue to decline after that. We will need to do much more in evangelism and church planting at home and abroad to reverse this trend. Does this need stir you to get involved in reaching the young at home or overseas?

We have come to rely on paid "surrogate servants" to serve in our place. The problem is that there are not nearly enough paid pastors, youth workers, Christian educators, missionaries or development workers to address these growing needs in our world today and tomorrow. Unless we remember that as disciples we are all called into active mission we could miss God's best for us and many of those in need could miss discovering how much God cares about their lives.

In search of a biblical theology of vocation

Why do so few of us have any time for witness or service? The most obvious answer is that many of us have given our first allegiance to the aspirations of Boom City . . . getting ahead in our jobs and in the consumer culture. But there are other reasons for our declining involvement that include a great deal of confusion regarding a biblical view of vocation.

Decoding the two-track view of vocation

In December 2001 we spoke at the InterVarsity Christian Fellowship's Urbana Missions Conference. The leaders in IVCF do a great job of challenging 20,000 college students from all over the United States and Canada to become world Christians and to consider God's mission call on their lives. However, many of the young people we talked to were getting another message that didn't come from the speakers, or the leaders at Urbana, but primarily from their own traditional church backgrounds. What they hear is that there are two totally different vocational tracks. The first track is to "obey God" completely, forget their colleges studies and career plans and simply go overseas as traditional unskilled missionaries. The second track is to be less than faithful, complete college, get a job and simply help support their friends who made the "higher choice" to be missionaries.

Speaking at Mission '98 in Korea we ran into another version of this two-track approach to vocation. The church in Korea has one of the most rapidly growing missions programmes in the world. At Mission '98 the expectation was that perhaps 10 per cent of the 5,000 college students in attendance would go into some form of world mission after graduation. The remaining 90 per cent who stayed at home were not expected to be actively involved in ministry at all. The church's unstated expectation for the second group was that they would simply get a job in one of Korea's large corporations, invest most of their waking hours at work and show up at church as their work schedule permitted. For this group allegiance to the workplace clearly comes first and with no expectation by church leaders that they would set aside time during the week for witness and service. I am sure these hardworking young Koreans do pray and provide support for their friends who made the "higher choice" too, but are they missing the best that God has for them?

We tried to help both these groups of eager young people realize that as followers of Jesus Christ there aren't two tracks. There is only one track. All followers of Christ are called into active witness and service to advance the purposes of God's kingdom . . . not just the full-time servants. Of course, becoming a missionary is one way to advance God's purposes. But as we explained to the young people at Urbana they don't have to turn their back on their educational preparation or their professional interests to become a missionary.

Decoding "your job is automatically your Christian vocation"

With the two-track model some have settled for a dualism in which "full-time Christian workers" seem to exist on a higher plane than the rest of us. However, there is another troubling view of Christian vocation that is also widely embraced. Simply stated this view insists that whatever we do for work is automatically our biblical vocation. A few years ago Tom was worshipping at a megachurch on the west coast of America. During a service on Christian vocation the pastor invited all 3,500 members to join him in a mass commissioning service. He instructed them to place their right hand on the left shoulder of the person next to them. Then he led them in a commissioning prayer for that person on their left.

Obviously the pastor was attempting to communicate that there aren't two tracks: the full-time servants and everyone else. But Tom struggled at several levels. First, most of the congregation had never met the person they were commissioning and had absolutely no idea of what they did for work. Second, the pastor clearly communicated the message that our job is automatically our Christian vocation. Unless you work in the pornography industry or run an escort service, whatever you do to earn income is automatically your Christian vocation. This viewpoint comes out of a Reformed view of life and work in which Luther affirmed that all we do is to the glory of God. While we certainly share Luther's affirmation we wouldn't share the conclusion that accompanies it . . . that whatever we do for work is necessarily our Christian vocation.

The view of work as vocation comes out of a theology of creation in which all work is seen as simply helping God subdue what is left of the natural order. As Tom wrote in *Mustard Seed vs McWorld*, we are not sure that helping Bill Gates subdue his few remaining competitors is anything like working with God to subdue the larger natural order.[9] Our second problem with this view of vocation is that it overlooks the fact that a number of those first disciples quit their jobs to follow their Christian vocations. Providing fish for families living in Galilee was certainly a part of the creation mandate. But Peter and James left their nets because Jesus called them to a new vocation that had a very specific kingdom focus, "to catch men".

A major weakness with this view of work as Christian vocation is that it only operates from a theology of creation and fails to consider a theology of the kingdom as well. Theologian Miroslav Volf insists that developing "a theology of work simply within the framework of the doctrine of creation" isn't adequate. He believes that a theology of work must also be seen in light of God's "new creation" which looks forward to God's restoration of all things at the coming of God's kingdom. The other view of vocation inadvertently justifies the status quo of the present global economic order instead of seeking to challenge and transform it.[10]

We share Volf's concern that this view tends to unconsciously assume that the agendas of the larger economic order and the agendas of specific corporations are identical to God's agenda for the human future. Any careful study of the kingdom purposes of God reflects a very different sense of intention for the future than that promoted by the architects of the Boom City project. This new global economy is constructed to persuade people everywhere to ratchet up our appetites for more. It is constantly trying to appeal to our greed, covetousness and self-interest to keep the economy growing. Aren't these goals consonant with the goals of God's kingdom?

We are all wired into the present economic reality and there is no way to move out of Boom City. There is also no biblical basis we know of to define whatever we do for work as automatically a Christian vocation. Volf observes that "The reduction of vocation to employment . . . contributed to the modern fateful elevation of work to the status of religion."[11] For many Western Christians vocation and occupation have become synonymous and some do pursue their labour with almost religious zeal. But there are ways we can express God's kingdom where we work.

Considering a third way . . . a vision for whole-life vocation

As we have seen the two-track approach to vocation tends to divorce our work from our Christian faith and contributes to the dualistic discipleship that is undermining our witness in society. And the view that our job is automatically our Christian vocation doesn't seem to be supported by scripture. The central theme of *Living on Purpose* is that we are persuaded the Bible calls us all to incarnate God's kingdom in every part of our lives in community including doing what Jesus did and making God's mission purposes our purposes too.

Joining Jesus in putting first things first
Remember Jesus stood up in his hometown and read his mission statement aloud out of Isaiah 61, "The Spirit of the

Lord is on me, because he has anointed me to preach good news to the poor. He has sent me to proclaim freedom for the prisoners and recovery of sight for the blind, to release the oppressed, to proclaim the year of the Lord's favor" (Luke 4:18–19). After he read it he sat down and said something quite astonishing, "Today this scripture is fulfilled in your hearing." What it meant for him to be the Messiah of God was not only a total commitment to God but to the mission purposes of God. Apparently John wasn't convinced that Jesus was indeed the Messiah of God so he sent two of his disciples to Jesus to seek convincing evidence that he was indeed the Chosen One of God. What proof did Jesus offer John's disciples? "Go back and report to John what you have seen and heard: The blind receive sight, the lame walk, those who have leprosy are cured, the deaf hear, the dead are raised, and the good news is preached to the poor" (Luke 7: 22). The proof Jesus offered that he was the Messiah of God was that he was actively devoting his life to advancing God's compassionate purposes.

In the first century it doesn't appear that witness and service were an optional part of discipleship as they seem to be today. And a little word on the job for Jesus wouldn't cut it. Sharing the good news in word and deed seemed to be an integral part of their more vital whole-life faith as followers of Christ. In fact historians tell us that one of the major reasons the early church grew so rapidly was because of the way the church reached out in love and the power of the Holy Spirit.

Rene Padilla in his important book *Mission Between the Times* provides one of the best definitions of the integration of word and deed mission, "Both evangelism and social responsibility can be understood only in light of the fact that in Jesus Christ the kingdom of God has invaded history and is both a present reality and a future hope . . . it is God's redemptive power released in history, bringing good news to the poor, freedom to the prisoners, sight to the blind and liberation to the oppressed."[12] Where should we start in our quest to be good news in our world?

Listening to a virtual Jesus calling us to seek first a coming kingdom

Join me for a moment and imagine that we are all 21 again and about to graduate from college. We sit together in the auditorium waiting for the graduation speech. We are jazzed. Somehow, through virtual reality, the administration has arranged for Jesus of Nazareth to be our speaker. We all hush as Jesus appears on the screen. We listen carefully . . . I mean this is Jesus speaking at our graduation. Awesome! He makes a strong start by reminding us how much God loves us. But then he explains how much God also loves our world and particularly some very unpleasant people. People around us begin to squirm a bit. Then Jesus makes some suggestions for our lives after graduation that frankly aren't very practical. He tells us not to sweat about where we get money not just for cool things but even the basics like food and clothes. He is clearly not in touch with the real world.

Jesus actually has the audacity to suggest that if we give our first priority to making a difference then our basic needs will be provided for. He concludes by asking God to bring his kingdom on earth like it is in heaven . . . through our lives. And we are out of there. Fortunately my pastor has a much more practical take on this whole business of life after graduation. He said there is a businessman in our church who could help me find a really good paying job. He also knows a dealer who will help me get a really good loan for a new BMW I promised myself. He knows I am committed to God and the church and all that stuff. I assured him that I will show up at church when I can and give as I am able . . . just like my parents. Cool!

What is life decision No. 1?

Of course this scenario is tongue in cheek. But it isn't as far removed from the real world as you might imagine. Frankly, we find in working with college grads, Christians and non-Christians, that there is virtually no difference at all in terms of priorities for life after graduation. For all the talk about "Lordship discipleship" everyone knows the drill. Life decision No. 1 is about getting the job, the house, the car and the cool stuff. Then after all the furniture of our lives is neatly in place we try to work in a little faith . . . which is getting tougher and tougher. Sound familiar?

When we work with Christian college students we tell them that life decision No. 1 is not where to work, where to live or even who to marry. We believe that life decision No. 1, for all generations, is "How does God want to use my life to make a difference in the world?" Then we make all other life decisions in light of life decision No. 1 including where to work, how long to work and where to live. We really suspect Jesus was deadly serious when he called us to seek first the kingdom and trust God for our beans and jeans. So how do we find God's best? By putting God's mission purposes at the very centre of our lives.

Exploring ways to put first things first

Putting first things first in the workplace

What are specific practical examples of what it might look like to put God's purposes at the centre of our lives like Jesus and those first disciples did? Of course our prime hours are usually those devoted to work. We work to support ourselves and our families. We work, under the creation mandate, to provide for the needs of the larger society. We work to utilize our gifts and give expression to our interests. For some going to work is the thrill of the contest and it is all about winning and beating out the competition. For others work is a place of companionship and community. For still others work is simply a place one endures in order to make enough money to survive.

Bob Buford, in his helpful book *Half Time*, states that most people spend the first half of their lives at work pursuing success. The invitation of his book is for those who have achieved success in the workplace to use the second half of their lives to pursue significance. He views the quest for success as an altogether positive pursuit that has its time and season in our lives. "The good life, in the most positive use of that term, is the result of a healthy desire to be successful. . . . When it is all said and done, our success will be pretty empty unless it has included a corresponding degree of significance – much of what we do in the first half is not imbued with the presence of the eternal."[13] For those in their middle years his book offers an important challenge to use the second half of their lives to find a way to make their life count for the kingdom. My question is: why should we wait until we are middle aged to invest our life in pursuit of significance?

Mark Markiewicz, a leader in YWAM UK, received a very unusual invitation from the Speaker of the House of Parliament in Kazakstan a couple of years ago. Mark was asked to bring people to Kazakstan who could help establish responsible businesses in their new free-market economy. The request caused Mark to do some research on the influence of the gospel on entrepreneurship in Britain during the last few centuries. He was amazed at what he found. A group of Christian grocers studied scripture together and out of their study drafted 12 principles that included using honest scales. Over time other grocers also started using fair weights and measures and placing the needs of their customers above their own self-interest to be able to do business.

Jesse Boots, the son of the man who founded Boots Chemist, was appalled that his father's shops coated herbal cures with gold leaf and served only very wealthy clients. Out of Christian conscience, when Jesse took over the business, he found ways to make pharmaceuticals as inexpensively as possible so they could be available to the poor who had no access to drugs. Boots is still a thriving business today. Wouldn't it have been a shame if Jesse had waited until he was middle aged to make his life count?[14]

Merle and Randy Beck are a father and son team who are determined to bring their faith to bear in their business entrepreneurship in China. Their company, Style Mark Inc., produces urethane millwork products for commercial and residential markets. In 1997 they opened their first plant in Yantai, China. They now produce a good product at a fair value. They also find that numbers of workers from other businesses in the region are clamouring to work for them because they pay wages well above the state-owned businesses, provide housing allowances, medical and pension benefits. As an expression of their Christian faith they also take time for a very personal interest in their employees' problems. Merle said "it's a pretty good feeling to be able to sit around a table, eating hundred-year-old eggs or sucking silkworms, and establishing rapport with the people . . . and have them call you Brother or Sister."[15]

Putting first things first by changing our careers into our callings

For those who do not have the freedom to express their faith through their immediate work situation there are other options. In Gerald Sittser's thoughtful book *The Will of God as a Way of Life,* he offers some very helpful insights on how we might transform our careers into callings. For example Sittser states "Selling insurance is a career, determined by the size of the policies sold, whether people need the insurance or not; helping people become good stewards of their resources is a calling."[16]

Gary, a friend of ours who is news director for a major Oregon TV station, makes a concerted effort to report good news every day that reflects some of the positive changes taking place in the community to provide glimpses of the shalom of God. Mark, a 20-year-old, left a very high-paying job in Silicon Valley to help Christian organizations develop high quality web pages. Many people have wonderful training or experience and they could, with a little creativity, transform a career preoccupied with the pursuit of success to a calling focused on making a difference. Is God nudging you like Mark to consider a major change or perhaps a major juggling of your life priorities so you can put first things first?

Putting first things first through creative stewardship of our lives

At the turn of the last century Tom's grandparents were starting out their lives farming in southern Idaho. They worked 12- to 16-hour days, seven days a week, as most of our forbears did, to provide a subsistence living for themselves and their five children. One of the new opportunities of the times in which we live is that many of us can live very comfortably on a lot less than a full-time income. How many hours a week do you need to work for your needs? Ron Johansen is a cardiologist in Minneapolis whose sense of calling has led him increasingly towards medical missions. He has cut back from a killer schedule to only four days a week and eight months out of the year to free up time to work in Africa with Missions Moving Mountains.

In Seattle, Amy found another way to put first things first. She followed the formula in the national best seller *Your Money or Your Life*.[17] Amy worked very hard for seven years, lived very simply and put almost her entire income into long-term investments. She put away enough essentially to retire early as a 35-year-old single woman. She lives comfortably but not lavishly in a large home with other people who share her values. Now her time is totally her own and she has time to pursue her calling as a full-time volunteer with Habitat for Humanity instead of simply punching a clock. She is having the time of her life.

Putting first things first through creative use of our free time

If you can't find a way to make a kingdom difference through your work, change your career into a calling or do early retirement, there are still ways you can make a kingdom difference with your life. Most of us could free up at least two hours a week for others. For example, a group of singles in an urban

Presbyterian church became very concerned about the needs of single mothers in their church and community. They started a ministry called Los Banditos. The members of Los Banditos devoted an evening a week to the ministry. Through the pastoral staff they learned about the needs of these mothers and their children. Then they made anonymous deliveries of food and clothing to needy families or offered child care or employment opportunities. Their delivery was always signed "Los Banditos have struck again!"

While speaking at a church in Bellevue, Washington recently Tom stated that what bonds Christian families together is exactly the same as what bonds those outside the church . . . we consume together in the Boom City Mall. He said, "I have never seen a church anywhere in North America that enables families to be bonded together in ministry to others." He challenged families in that church to free up an evening a week for others. When he came back to the church six weeks later the church hadn't changed. But one woman told him, "We are doing it!" He asked, "What are you doing?" She replied, "As a result of your challenge we have changed our timestyle and freed up Wednesday night for ministry. We are helping seniors who are housebound with their chores so they aren't forced to leave their homes. Because of what you shared I take my two little preschoolers with me. They don't watch mum work. They are right down scrubbing the floor alongside me." What kind of kids would we raise up if instead of 18 years of high-indulgence living in the suburbs they were involved with mum and dad working to bring "sight to the blind, release to the captives, good news to the poor"?

Tom received one of the most unusual thank you notes of his life from two remarkable kids, Tracy and Brent Anderson. They thanked him for the opportunity to live in Zaire for a year. Some 18 months before he received the note Tom spoke at a Free Methodist Church Tracy and Brent and their parents attended. He challenged parents to think about living in a third world culture for the sake of their kids. Apparently mum and dad Anderson took his words seriously. Dad asked for a year's leave of absence from the Christian school where he taught. He found a mission in Zaire that needed a teacher for a year. The Andersons signed up and away they went. The note from the kids thanked Tom for a chance to make new friends and experience another culture.

June and Brad have a strong sense of Christian calling to work with foster kids that no one wants. They provided a loving home for dozens of kids over the years and numbers of the kids became committed Christians who have never forgotten June and Brad's loving, patient parenting and their deep faith. God stirred Greg and Eydie's heart with a concern for at-risk kids struggling in our school system. They started tutoring sisters Zen and Nunisha, whose family had recently migrated from Ethiopia. Zen was 12 when Greg started tutoring her. She knew almost no English and was painfully shy. Greg relates that over the first year Zen came to life as she not only discovered poetry but also read her poems in class. One day out of the blue Zen asked Greg, "Why do you take time to tutor me?" Greg was taken aback by the question. He responded honestly, "I started tutoring you because I am a Christian but I continued to tutor you because we are friends." Recently Greg and Eydie had the opportunity to celebrate Zen's graduation from the University of Washington with a degree in English Literature. Do you have any doubt as to whether Greg and Eydie found some of the best God had for their lives?

Dreaming new dreams and birthing new possibilities

Imagine for just a minute what would happen in your church or ours if every member were involved in active witness or service at least two hours a week in the larger community. Can you visualize the potential difference it could make? In *Wake Up Your Dreams* Walt Kallestead writes, "We are made in the image of the Creator of dreams – the ultimate Dream Maker. . . . The ability to dream is a God given legacy. What an incredible

Off Ramp No. 14
Putting your mission statement into action

Now it is your opportunity to discover personally that the good life of God is the life given away.

1. Take at least two hours for this final off ramp. Take out your personal mission statement, your goals, and what you learned about ministries in your last off ramp and pray to God to show you possible new ways He can use your life to make a difference through your workplace, by transforming your career into a calling or freeing up a couple hours a week for witness or service.
2. Define as clearly as you can specific goals for the way God is calling you to make a difference either through re-focusing an existing ministry, joining a ministry or creating a new form of witness or service.
3. List the initial action steps you would need to actually take to put wheels under your mission statement and discover how God can use your life to make a difference.
4. Share your specific ministry focus and your initial action steps to get things rolling with your group or a friend. Ask them to pray with you for the empowerment of the Holy Spirit and ask them to call you each week for the next four weeks to see how you are going.

opportunity has been given us to be partners in creation, to dream to contribute, to accomplish amazing things."[18] He is right. God does invite us into creative partnership to dream new dreams and to find creative ways to improvise our lives in God's story. You have begun a very important journey towards *Living on Purpose* . . . living with significance.

The author of Hebrews urges us to follow Jesus by putting first things first and by remembering that there is a great company of witnesses praying for us and cheering us on. "Do you see what this all means – all these pioneers who blazed the way, all these veterans cheering us on? It means we'd better get on with it. Strip down and start running – and never quit! No extra spiritual fat, no parasitic sins. Keep your eyes on Jesus, who both began and finished this race we're in. Study how he did it. Because he never lost sight of where he was headed – that exhilarating finish in and with God . . ." Hebrews 12:1–2, *The Message*.

Notes

1. Paul Borthwick, *A Mind For Missions*, Colorado Springs: Nav Press, 1988, pp. 147–149.
2. Douglas LeBlanc, "Honest Prayer Beautiful Grace", *Christianity Today*, February 5, 2001, p. 77.
3. David Barrett ed.,*World Christian Encyclopedia*, New York: Barrett, Kurian, & Johnson, 2001, p. 6 and a forthcoming publication on "World Christian Trends" by David Barrett.
4. Christopher Wren, "World Needs to Add 500 Million Jobs in 10 Years, Report Says", *New York Times*, January 25, 2001, p. A13.
5. Tom Sine, *Mustard Seed vs. McWorld: Reinventing Life*, Grand Rapids: Baker Books, 1999, pp. 114–115. (UK edition: Monarch Books.)
6. "UK Four million children living in poverty", BBC News on line, http//news.bbc.co.uk/hi/English/uk/newsid_398000/398666.stm.
7. "Housing and Homelessness in England: the facts", Shelter website www.shelter.org.uk
8. Jonathan Alter, "The War on Addiction", *Newsweek*, February 12, 2001, pp. 34–43.
9. Tom Sine, p. 161.
10. Miroslav Volf, *Work in the Spirit: Toward a Theology of Work*, New York: Oxford University Press, 1991, pp. 101–102.
11. Volf, p. 109.
12. C. Rene Padilla, *Mission Between the Times: Essays on the Kingdom*, Grand Rapids: Eerdmans, 1985, p. 197.

13. Bob Buford, *Half Time: Changing Your Game Plan From Success to Significance*, Grand Rapids: Zondervan, 1994, p. 84.
14. Mark Markiewicz, "Business as Mission". Presented November 7, 1999, at a Symposium on Doing Mission Through Business, Seattle.
15. Wally Kroeker, "Mission on the Factory Floor", *The Marketplace*, January February 2000, pp. 11–12.
16. Gerald L. Sittser, *The Will of God as a Way of Life*, Grand Rapids: Zondervan, 2000, p. 72.
17. Joe Dominguez and Vicki Robin, *Your Money or Your Life: Transforming Your Relationship With Money and Achieving Financial Independence*, New York: Penguin Books, 1993.
18. Walt Kallestead, *Wake Up Your Dreams*, Grand Rapids: Zondervan, 1996, p. 30.

Living on Purpose: The Beginning

Looking back and looking forward

We have been on a journey together in this book to discover creative new ways we can respond to Jesus Christ's strong challenge to seek first the kingdom in our 24/7 world. We recognize that most of us struggle to keep our heads above water and the pressures of daily life are relentless. But we also recognize that we all want to pursue the best that God has for us. The problem is that most of us have very little idea how to connect our Sunday faith to our seven day a week life. Since we don't know how to make that connection, too often the aspirations and values of the Land of Illusions have more impact on shaping our life direction and values than our faith does.

This book has had a very simple mission. We have tried to present one practical way to enable you to connect your Sunday faith to your life, seven days a week. If you have used this book as a workbook in a group or shared with some friends hopefully you have created that connection and begun to discover the best that God has for you. If you have then by now you have:

- Diagnosed some of the reasons for your hurry sickness;
- Decoded some of the seductive values of the Land of Illusions;
- Gained a clearer sense of God's loving purposes for a people and a world;
- Written a beginning mission statement showing how God might use your life to advance those purposes;
- Drafted goals that describe how you might give expression to that mission statement in every area of your life;

LIVING ON PURPOSE: THE BEGINNING 187

- Reinvented your timestyle and lifestyle to more authentically reflect your faith in your weekly rhythm and freed up more of your time and money to invest in the advance of God's new order;
- Created specific ways you could invite God to use your life to make a difference for God's kingdom either through your work hours or your discretionary time;
- Explored ways you can find people to join you in new forms of community that both incarnationally reflect something of God's new order and provide the support and accountability we all need to be whole-life disciples, stewards and servants.

We would love to hear about your experiences in seeking to put God's purposes first in your life. Share your stories at msasines@cs.com or write to us at Mustard Seed Associates, Box 45867, Seattle, WA 98145. We will share some of your stories on our web page: www.msainfo.org where you can meet other Christians from all over the world who are also finding ways to put God's purposes first in their lives and communities of faith.

Some other web resources that might be helpful to you in your quest are:

- Hunger issues www.worldhunger.org and www.tearfund.org
- Institute for Global Ethics www.globalethics.org
- For people standing tall and sticking their neck out for the poor www.giraffe.org
- For international stewardship www.internationalsteward.org
- For practical stewardship www.turningpoint.com and www.thegoodsteward.com
- www.stewardshipservices.org Stewardship services works to maximize good stewardship amongst Christians, churches and Christian organizations in the UK
- Cohousing resources www.cohousing.org
- For young leaders www.youngleaders.org and www.joshgen.org and www.tribalgen.org

- www.adbusters.org – Adbusters is the best publication we
  have found that with humour assists people to decode the
  messages of our new global economy
- www.wfs.org – the World Futures Society provides information on social and technological trends that are shaping our
  future
- www.christian-research.org.uk and
  www.ukchristianhandbook.org.uk – for trends likely to
  impact the church now and in the future
- www.barna.org tracks demographic and church-related
  trends in the U.S.
- www.simpleliving.org Alternatives for Simple Living equips
  people of faith to challenge consumerism, live justly and celebrate responsibly

In his book *The Forever Feast* Dr Paul Brand tells the story of
an Arabic Baptist Church in Israel that beautifully illustrates
the richness of our sacramental life together in community.
"When they come together, each member brings handful of
grains of wheat. It may be from one's own field, or from their
personal supplies at home. As they enter the church, they each
pour grains into a common pot. When all have come, and while
the worship goes on, the pot is taken to the kitchen and somebody quickly grinds the wheat in a stone mill, mixes in water
and salt, and kneads the flour into a loaf. It is put into the
already-heated oven and baked.

"By the time the service is finished and the church moves into
the celebration of the Lord's supper and the breaking of bread,
the loaf is ready. As each member breaks off his own portion,
he or she is sharing grains of flour from every member of the
church. When asked why they do this, one member replied, 'As
individual seeds we are each alone and separate from each
other. Only when we are broken into flour and baked together
can we experience full fellowship.'"[1]

Only as our separate seeds merge together can we discover
the best that God has for us . . . to become a part of God's story

and a sacrament of God's love to a world. "Welcome to the celebration and adventure of the good news" that God is redeeming a people and transforming a world. "The Mustard Seed Conspiracy begins with you and me . . . It begins with a new joyous celebration of life, relationships, and vocation, making ourselves much more available to the loving initiatives of God."[2] It begins by making God's purposes our purposes and discovering life with a difference.

Notes

1. Dr Paul Brand, *The Forever Feast*, Ann Arbor: Vine Books, 1993, pp. 193–194.
2. Tom Sine, *The Mustard Seed Conspiracy*, Waco: Word Books, 1981, p. 237.